****

Death ... and the lessons i learned

Discovering inspiration, love, acceptance, peace, and spiritual growth in the difficult moments of life

****

Louise Smith

Library and Archives Canada Cataloguing in Publication
L. Smith

ISBN 978-1-926626-49-9

Printed and Bound by First Choice Books
www.firstchoicebooks.ca

Printed in Canada

Photo Credits;

Front cover photo:
Sky at Gorman Lake, Ontario, copyright 2006 Sydney Smith
Back cover photo:
Mountain biking in Calcdon, Ontario, copyright 2008 Janis Jarvis
Pen and ink drawing:
'The Journey', artist Richard Smith, copyright 2009

****

This book is dedicated to all who have passed before me. I look forward to the day my lessons are complete and we meet again on the Other Side.

Much love,
Louise

****

Foreword

Asha Frost HD

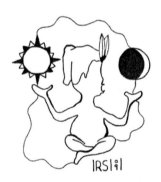

It has been my experience that death can create a range of emotions for the beings on this planet. As a Shaman, I have worked through healing my own issues around death and have been taken through my own death rites. Thus, the inevitability of death no longer haunts me. However, in my everyday practice I can see how it haunts the lives of others. This beautiful book outlines this very concept and it does so in a healed way.

As we go deep inside to heal our wounds, we come out on the other end in the light. As we recognize what we need to learn, we trust that everything works out exactly as it should. *Death... and the lessons i learned* illustrates these teachings in a way that we can all understand. It reminds us about the importance of living in the moment, of knowing thyself and of trusting that indeed, there is a greater power working behind the scenes of our lives.

In the world of New Age and Spirituality there is a need for rooting, for grounding. This book brings us back to the earthly plane where we need to live out the teachings, walk our talk and heal what needs to be healed. Using real life examples with interjections of humor and healing, *Death... and the lessons i learned* offers an all-encompassing view of death. It is in the surrender, the acceptance and the embrace where healing occurs. If we are able to heed these teachings, we realize that an experience with death can ultimately bring us back to life, a life that we were all destined to live.

…Asha

Introduction

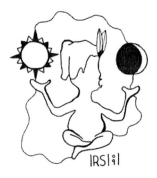

Grief is an interesting aspect of life. It takes us by the scruff of our neck and shakes us uncontrollably. We humans would normally avoid such a peril at all costs, yet it is an essential element of life that every one of us must experience.

Grief and spiritual growth walk hand in hand. With every loss we are given opportunities to grow, learning life lessons that move us forward on our soul's journey. Some of us excel at learning the lessons. Others, without realizing it, do everything in their power to avoid the difficult elements of grief and, as such, miss the lessons all together. As a result they repeat the cycle again and again as the lessons are put in front of them any number of ways until they finally get it.

There is no limit to the number of lessons we need to learn or the types of loss we will grieve. We may lose family, friends, jobs, homes, careers, relationships, power and even our dignity.

In each of these losses one element remains the same. We must journey through all five stages of grief before we can release the final remnants of the cycle, walk out from under the black cloud and move forward on our life path. The five stages of grief are:

1. Denial and isolation,
2. Anger,
3. Bargaining,
4. Depression, and
5. Acceptance.

How long we spend in each of the stages will differ with each person and each loss. There is no rule on what an appropriate period of time in each stage should be.

I have experienced the loss of close family members, and yet zoomed through to sit comfortably in stage five before others seemed to realize there even were stages of grief.

Yet other times I have held on, gripping the walls of one of the first four stages for what seemed an eternity. In hindsight I will tell you that moments I dug in my heels were the times I refused to acknowledge there was a bigger lesson for me to learn.

In the difficult moments of our lives, when lessons are presented to us, we *must* acknowledge and learn them to complete the stages of grief, finish that cycle and move on.

This book is for all those who have lost a person, job, love, career, pet or other cherished piece of their lives. It is a book about spiritual growth, inspiration, love, acceptance, peace, and contentment.

I only ask that you read the pages with an open heart, looking for the parallels to your own life lessons. My hope is that you acknowledge these lessons, complete the cycle and move on peacefully in the journey of your life.

****

We are not human beings on a spiritual journey. We are spiritual beings on a human journey.

… Stephen Covey

****

One

A Gun in My Back

Lesson Learned

Sometimes it's essential to keep my big mouth shut!

When I was twenty-one I was a travel agent. I loved seeing the world and at that time the profession offered me incredible discounts to travel to the four corners of the earth, which was by far my favorite aspect of the industry.

At a sales conference in Atlanta, Georgia, my girlfriend and I had won free tickets with the now long-gone and defunct Eastern Airlines to anywhere in South America we wanted to go. Having already planned a two-month backpacking trip through Europe for ten months down the road, we decided to limit our expenses and settled on two weeks and two countries.

Off to Peru and Bolivia we went.

Although I was born to immigrants and had traveled a fair amount as a youngster, I was without a doubt a typical twenty-one-year-old. You know what I mean. The type who think they have seen it all, done it all and believe that nothing bad could ever happen to them.

It really was a most incredible experience. I recall waking

up in Machu Picchu, high atop the Andes mountain range, with an early morning mist gently drifting in over the tops of the green, lush mountains that stood like pillars pointing to the heavens, thinking that I had just experienced a gift from God.

Visiting ancient Inca ruins like Saqsawaman and Ollantaytambo jetted me back to a time long before our land in North America was even discovered. It was invigorating to see these ancient masterpieces and made me feel small and insignificant in my contributions to the world thus far.

I remember being warned not to travel with large sums of money, for both the drug runners and authorities could mistake you for being on the other side. This was something I had told my own clients who were venturing into countries known for their illegal drug trade.

I ignored the warnings. None of that sort of thing really happened at home, in the land of the peaceful, easygoing, always honest Canadians, and I was a fun-loving gal who loved being the life of the party. I honestly didn't think anyone could mistake me for a drug lord involved in guerilla warfare.

To be on the safe side, though, I decided to carry my money in the form of hundred dollar denomination traveler's checks.

We hired guides in Lima, Peru, my girlfriend and I. It was the smartest decision I had ever made while traveling. We didn't speak Spanish, for one, and everyone seemed to operate with a different set of rules, so having our guides handle everything just made sense.

At one point our guides had to help us get on a flight from Lima to Cuzco so that we could visit the lost city, Machu Picchu. The airport for domestic flights was a surreal experience. First of all, the Peruvians always seemed to be yelling, pushing and shoving. Second, it would take bribery, not just a ticket, to get us on the plane.

Without a word of a lie, our guides walked us out on the

tarmac, past the check-in agents and security points to the portable stairs leading to the front door of the airplane. There were a zillion other people also trying to get on the plane. We had tickets. That didn't seem to matter.

Our guides were yelling and screaming and throwing money into the faces of those who appeared to be officials. They kept pushing us forward, up the stairs, closer and closer to the open door of the plane.

Money changed hands, but apparently not enough. The doors closed, the plane started to move away and we were left standing at the top of the portable staircase.

Our guides looked as us, shook their heads and said with a shrug that we'd have better luck on the next one. They suggested we head to their house for a coffee and rest before attempting another flight.

Two male guides. Two young girls. We probably should have been nervous, but they had been shuttling us around and doing our talking for over a week and we just out and out trusted them.

The house was nice, the Peruvian coffee incredibly great, and it was indeed good to relax in a quiet setting with our new friends who were nothing short of gentlemen. And they were right. The next flight was much more successful.

It was a trip of crazy experiences. More bizarre things happened in those two weeks than in the rest of our lives combined.

One time, we thought we were being kidnapped. I kid you not. We were sitting in the lobby of a hotel-type lodging, somewhere near Lake Titicaca, waiting for our new guide to come and get us. I'm not sure if it's still like that in Peru and Bolivia, but when we were there having guides usher us around was just the way it was done.

While waiting in the lobby, two strange men we had never seen before came up and without saying a word, quickly grabbed our suitcases and ran outside, throwing them onto a roof rack of a car. We bolted after them, trying to call for assistance from the sleepy gal at the makeshift reception desk.

Before we knew what was happening, one guy opened the back door and shoved us in, all the while saying something in Spanish. We landed on each other in a messy fashion and as we yelled no, no, no, the two guys in the front of the car just kept yelling back *sí, sí, sí*, and drove us away.

We made a pact, my girlfriend and I, in that back seat. As soon as the car came to a stop, be that a rolling one or a real one, we would open the doors and jump out. We wanted to do this before we were driven outside of the city. Before they had a chance to do whatever it was they were planning to do, the crazy-ass kidnappers.

The car stopped at an intersection. I bolted, and I mean bolted. I left the suitcase behind and barely even stopped long enough to make sure my girlfriend was coming. We ran helter skelter across the intersection and there in front of us, on the other side of the street, was a touring bus.

"Just make it to the bus!" I yelled. "Just make it to the bus!"

During this trip we had befriended a retired couple from Panama City, Panama. Catherine and Eddie. It seemed that everywhere we went they went too. The only difference was that they traveled first class and we didn't even have class.

I ran onto the bus, fear blazing in my eyes, hoping someone could help us. There standing in front of me, of all people, was Catherine. She grabbed me up in her arms and comforted me. Eddie did the same for my girlfriend.

Just when we were almost calm and ready to tell the story of our harrowing experience, we looked out the window. There were our two kidnapping-crazy-car-drivers walking in our direction.

They were sauntering towards the bus, our suitcases in tow, handing them over to the bus driver. They looked up at us gently nestled in the arms of our protectors and shook their heads like we were the craziest fare they had ever picked up.

Sure enough, our guide jumped on board the bus right then and the first question out of his mouth was whether the taxi he had sent picked us up okay. Seems he had given them our descriptions so that when they arrived at the hotel, they would know who we were right away.

Note to self. Learn at least a little of the native language of every country you visit.

Another time we were sitting on a school bus, traveling somewhere between Peru and Bolivia. I distinctly remember that I was reading the Sidney Sheldon book, *Master of the Game*. It was an incredible read and I was easily lost in the words that flowed across the pages.

All of a sudden, someone jerked me out of the absorbing plot. It was my girlfriend, yelling at me and pulling me down. I looked up from the pages. Everyone on the bus was lying on the floor while I sat up straight as an arrow, book in hand.

I looked out the window and noticed we had left the highway and were driving through a farmer's field. There, to my right, about 300 feet away, was a highway barricade built by crazy guerillas who were apparently threatening to shoot anyone who tried to continue along the highway.

The bus driver was now yelling at me to get down, or at least that's what I took his Spanish instructions to mean. I dropped to the floor, lost my page in the book and whispered with the few English-speaking people on board.

Unlike the fake kidnapping, turns out this crazy experience was real. They really were guerillas angry about something and ready to make their point, and shots really were fired at random. The bus driver thought the best course of action was to try to drive around them without being noticed.

A school bus. Lumbering through a farmer's field, in full view of the guerilla blockade. I agree it seemed a little odd that Mr. Bus Driver thought this might work, but I wasn't about to argue and no alternative came to mind.

Eventually the driver felt we were far enough past the barricade. He steered the bus back onto the road and we continued on our merry little way. We shook our heads in disbelief, my girlfriend and I, wondering if this was the norm for a life in South America.

The most terrifying experience of my life happened within two days of arriving on the continent. This was back with our airplane-bribing-gentlemen guides in Lima.

I wanted to change one of my hundred dollar traveler's checks into some cold hard Peruvian currency. My guide looked at the amount and cringed. He asked if I had anything smaller, to which I shook my head. Nodding slowly, he said we might have trouble.

The seriousness of his comment didn't really register in my twenty-one-year-old I-know-everything mind.

Leaving my girlfriend and her guide shopping, my guide and I headed to cash the traveler's check. We walked through an alley. That should have been my first clue. Up a set of rickety stairs. That should have been the second one. Into what my guide called an "official bank."

It was small, slightly larger than a North American two-piece bathroom. It smelled funny and was occupied by a guard at the door and a male teller seated behind an iron-gate barrier.

My guide talked to the teller as I stood still.

After a few minutes my guide instructed me to hand my traveler's check to the man sitting at the desk on the other side of the iron-gate barrier. I slipped the check through.

The iron-gate man looked at it and the yelling began.

Before I knew what was happening, the guard who was posted at the door we had entered through stepped in my direction and put the barrel of his machine gun to my back. I could feel the hard, cold steel digging into my spine.

My guide, watching this happen, started yelling in a newly intensified, fevered pitch.

I stood like a deer in the headlights, afraid that any

sudden movement might alarm the man at the other end of the barrel in my back.

The iron-gate man got to his feet, showing his growing anger, and yelled some more. Another official came busting through the door and pointed a machine gun at my guide.

My guide's angry words turned to soft, barely audible pleading. All the while I had absolutely no idea what was going on.

The iron-gate man yelled an instruction to my guide who, slowly and with a look of defeat in his eyes, shook his head. The man yelled again and whatever he said, he meant business. My guide looked at me with sorrow and told me to hand my passport over and put my hand through the opening of the iron-gate.

Slowly and carefully I did both.

The machine gun pushed further into my back, as if to make sure I followed the instructions. The iron-gate man grabbed my hand and before I knew it, I was being fingerprinted. For what I did not know, and although I had never been in this position before, it felt like I was being arrested.

My guide pleaded. Or at least I think he was pleading. The tone sounded desperate.

We stood like that for some time, how long I don't really know. It could have been minutes, but it felt like hours. I realized in that moment of standstill time that tears were rolling down my cheeks. The terror surging through my body was so intense I looked down to see if I had wet my pants. By the grace of God, I had not.

In that moment of absolute fear, I wondered if this was my time to die. It sure felt like it, so I whispered a silent prayer to God asking Him to take me quickly, before any pain hit my body. Before I figured out what was going on.

My guide, machine gun still pointed at him, continued to softly plead. I continued to be fingerprinted. A person from a back room had taken my passport and upon returning, spoke with a sense of ultimate authority. I have no idea what was said, but the machine gun in my back was slowly lowered. The iron-gate man dropped my hand in angry protest directed to the passport-holder. I pulled my hand away quickly, fingers still full of ink.

Money and my passport were shoved through the opening and iron-gate man started yelling again. My guide told me to quickly grab it before they changed their minds. I did – and in seconds we were down the rickety stairs and running through the streets.

About a block away we slowed down to a walk. I had a million questions to ask, but words didn't form and my mind wouldn't stop racing. I felt like I had somehow cheated death.

When we caught our breath, my guide explained what had just gone down.

Turns out the amount of money I was cashing, all one hundred dollars, was greater than two months salary for the average Peruvian. The officials surmised by this that I must have been a drug-runner.

My guide tried to explain that I was not, but there had been so many deaths in recent months from the drug trade that the officials were not taking any chances.

I asked if it was really as serious as it felt, back there, down the alley, with the iron-gate man and the machine guns. My guide told me yes. He told me that the only thing that saved me was the fact that I didn't utter a word.

He told me they are used to American drug-runners that pretend they don't speak Spanish as a method of hiding their true identity, but some things were said in that volley of screaming and yelling that should have made any Spanish-speaking individual speak up in defense.

Because I didn't seem to comprehend anything that was being said or going on, and my guide kept explaining that I was a tourist, a travel agent checking out their country for clients, they eventually decided to let me go.

I remember asking what would have happened to me, had it not turned out the way it did. My guide told me the arrest would have continued, they would have taken me immediately to prison and then it would have been in the hands of my Embassy to prove my innocence and get me out.

Thank God I kept my big mouth shut. I learned that day that words are not always necessary and sometimes it's best to let others do the talking.

I didn't die, but somehow the experience felt like a death to me. The know-it-all twenty-one-year-old girl no longer existed and a new, much wiser and more careful woman emerged.

It was a remarkable holiday. Although the check-cashing experience goes down in my books as the most harrowing day of my life, I really did love the continent, the people and the history that told its stories in everything we saw and did.

The lesson was learned.

The cycle complete.

I moved on in my journey of life.

****

The fear of death flows from the fear of life. A man who lives fully is prepared to die at any time.

… Mark Twain

****

Two

Best Friend's Brother

Lesson Learned

Death can make the closest of friends feel awkward.

There is no other moment in life where someone can feel so absolutely awkward and out of place than in the moment of death.

The first time I was acutely aware of my inability to know what was right to say or do was back in high school.

After a difficult family move where I was uprooted from the only life I had ever known, I finally, almost a full year later, developed friendships with girls somewhat like me.

They were my saving grace, my new girlfriends. We partied, laughed and did things that we now hope our own children stay away from. The old adage "it was the best of times and the worst of times" rang true for my final two years of high school.

One of my best friends had an older brother who was a star on the high school basketball team. High school sports in Canada are absolutely nothing like they are in the United States. We're lucky if there is a set of bleachers in the gymnasium for the odd soul who might wander past during a game and decide to take a rest and watch for a spell.

Although my girlfriend and I weren't into displaying affection for our siblings, we did stop by the gym periodically to watch her brother play. Boy did he love to play.

The news came as a shock.

He and the rest of the team were driving home in various cars from a game in a neighboring town. A drunk driver veered on the road, crashing into the car my friend's brother was in. He was killed instantly.

Our school went into mourning. His team, having lost a star player, went into shock. My friend understandably did not return to class immediately.

I had never felt so awkward in my life. I didn't know what to say to her, nor did I know how to act. I never went to her home, nor did I phone her again until after she returned to class.

My first opportunity to see her was at the funeral. Not knowing what to do, I went by myself. I sat in the back, looking left then right, and then left again, hoping the actions of others would guide me in what I was supposed to do.

Finally, at the end of the service my friend walked by and stopped in front of me. I whispered, "hey." She whispered the same back. I shifted uncomfortably in my spot, avoiding eye contact as much as possible. I shook my head a few times, hoping the action would release the words that seemed stuck somewhere deep inside me, miles away from being able to come out.

Eventually she smiled uncomprehendingly, turned and walked out of the funeral home. I waited until it was my row's turn to exit. Having absolutely no experience with what I should do next, I stepped quickly in the direction of my parents' car, got in and drove home.

That was it. That was all I could do or say in that moment of death. Once she returned to school and we started back to our normal routine of friendship, we did talk about his death and how hard it was. She even took the opportunity to ask me why I hadn't come out to the house following the service. I told her it was because I had no idea what I was supposed to do.

Over the years I have seen this type of reaction many times. People stumble and say the wrong thing. Or they say something hurtful that in their mind was anything but.

I've seen people avoid friends and family after a death, obviously not knowing how to react or what to say.

On the other side of that road, I have seen people send cards, make calls and get involved in the death-related activities of the family when they themselves are merely an acquaintance at best. Sometimes this behavior is met with gratitude but other times feels intrusive and adds stress to the grieving family.

If I learned any glaringly apparent lesson from the death of my friend's brother, it's that awkwardness often hits those affected by death. And that's okay.

There is no manual on how to respond to shocking news of the passing of a loved one, let alone the loved one of a friend. Everyone needs something different and there is no way you can know in advance what that might be.

Because of this, I have learned that whatever we do or say is okay. It's all we know. Although it may inadvertently hurt the grieving individual in that moment, they too need to know that death is difficult and we are doing the best we can.

For the grieving person to stay stuck on what someone did or didn't do only holds them back from healing. And rather than moving forward on their soul journey, it keeps them stuck in a holding pattern trying to make sense of something that never will make sense.

Just the same, for those who move through the death of a friend's loved one in an awkward manner, they can't blame themselves for not knowing what to do or say. It's okay to be lost a little in those moments.

Someone should write just one rule about death to help

people know what to do. It should simply say, "Anything and everything you do is okay."

I am glad that all those years ago I had the chance to talk with my friend about the death of her brother after the initial shock of it all had passed. It allowed me to express my awkwardness as well as my deepest condolences for her unbearable loss.

It also allowed me to learn a lesson about death, a lesson that would carry me through the decades of my life that followed.

The lesson was learned.

The cycle complete.

I moved on in my journey of life.

****

The idea of death, the fear of it, haunts the human animal like nothing else; it is a mainspring of human activity - designed largely to avoid the fatality of death, to overcome it by denying in some way that it is the final destiny of man.

… Ernest Becker

****

Three

Five in One

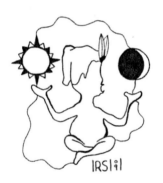

Lesson Learned

*We are not invincible – stupid decisions can lead to
catastrophic results.*

Teenagers do crazy, idiotic, stupid things. They just do.
Lord knows I did my fair share when I was that age.

My teenage life was during the days when no one seemed
to give a rat's ass about drinking and driving. Back then
everyone I knew went out and partied and drove home with
one hand covering an eye so the double vision was reduced.

This behavior wasn't reserved for just the bad kids, or the
ones that hung out with the druggies around the smoking area
outside of the school. It was pretty much everyone. The smart
kids, or browners as they were called then. The jocks. The
weed-smoking dopers. The partiers. Everyone but the non-
drinking Christian kids and they represented less than 1% of
the school population.

It didn't get any better when I headed off to college. I
have stories that would make my mother shake with anger
and want to ground me even now, regardless of the fact that I
am in my mid-forties and these crazy events happened nearly

thirty years ago.

We didn't learn. That's the scary part. Something would happen to a friend of ours, or a kid in our school or a neighboring school, and we'd all shiver with relief that it wasn't us. They'd get caught and be grounded. Or they'd get pulled over and lose their license. Sometimes, the odd time, they would be in a car accident.

But out we'd go, drinking and driving once again.

It wasn't a rebellious thing, the drinking and driving. It wasn't something we did because our parents told us not too. Many parents did it too, although I highly doubt my parents were ever guilty of this sin.

But many of my friends' parents did. I can remember getting into a car with a few dads who carried a "traveler," a beer that was safety tucked between their legs as they drove. No one seemed to care one way or another.

It was just something everyone did and no one thought the wiser. There was no MADD (Mothers Against Drunk Driving) then. There were no media campaigns warning us against the perils that lurked in the bottom of a bottle when the car keys were attached.

But now and then, every once in a while, something serious happened and it shook our world.

When I was fifteen, my father transferred from a small, rural community in Northwestern Ontario to the mega-busy suburbs of Toronto. That move devastated me in more ways than one.

I left behind my best friend. She was the one person who had stood by me through thick and thin, the one person I felt was my soul sister.

I also left behind the only life I knew. Although we had moved many times during my early childhood, we had settled in that particular town when I was six years old and stayed firmly planted until I was in the tenth grade. Trust me, moving a teenager during her high school years is not something I recommend.

To make matters worse, the summer following our move I convinced my parents to let me go back to stay with my best friend. I missed her and the town greatly.

During those weeks I fell in love for the first time in my life, with a boy who had just finished school. I was way too young to understand what love really was, and at that time I had no clue how deep my feelings went.

I sure figured it out, though. When I got home and started the second last year of my high school life, I found myself pining more than ever for my girlfriend, the town I adored and the boy who'd stolen my heart.

One evening the phone rang as I sat quietly watching TV with my parents. It was my girlfriend from up north. Through tears of shock and dismay, she recounted how five of our girlfriends had just died tragically in a car accident.

As the story goes, they were all out partying in a smaller town, about 30km to the west. True to the typical small-town teenager habits of the time, they were hammered. Drunker than skunks. They had been drinking most of the evening and although they may have seemed fine to their friends, they had far too much alcohol in their system to get behind a wheel and drive.

But they did. They got into the vehicle after deciding which was the most able to drive. Shortly after turning onto the two-lane highway headed back towards their town, they crossed the centre line and hit a transport truck head on. All five of my friends were killed instantly. I can only hope they never saw it coming.

The truck driver survived. I can't imagine what hell he was thrown into after that nightmare occurred. Drunken teenagers never think of that part.

In a small town like that it was as though royalty had died. Everyone went into mourning. The entire population of 6,700 grieved the senseless death of five beautiful souls who were far too young to go.

Sometimes death wakes us up.

We are not invincible. There is no law that states every person should live until they are ninety. There is nothing in writing that tells us we will live forever if we make the right choices and never make mistakes. Still, an overwhelming loss like this should make anyone stop and think.

Did every teenager affected by that death refrain from ever drinking and driving again? I doubt it. That wasn't the kind of era I grew up in. We were all fools then, unaware of the perils of driving with alcohol coursing through our veins. It was a different time.

Different time or not, I certainly learned a lesson. As much as I wanted to blame the deaths on this or that or someone else, I couldn't. As much as I was angry and tried to blame our move to the city as the reason I was not there to help my friends make a better choice that night, it was what it was. The result of a stupid decision to get behind the wheel while buzzed on booze. From then on I knew that in the blink of an eye, a life, my life, could be over if I made that same mistake.

The lesson was learned.

The cycle complete.

I moved on in my journey of life.

****

Amazing Grace

Amazing Grace! How sweet the sound
That saved a wretch like me!
I once was lost, but now am found:
Was blind, but now I see.

'Twas grace that taught my heart to fear,
And grace my fears relieved;
How precious did that grace appear
The hour I first believed.

Through many dangers, toils and snares,
I have already come;
'Tis grace hath brought me safe thus far,
And grace will lead me home.

The Lord has promised good to me,
His word my hope secures;
He will my Shield and Portion be,
As long as life endures.

Yea, when this flesh and heart shall fail,
And mortal life shall cease,
I shall progress within the veil,
A life of joy and peace.

When we've been there ten thousand years,
Bright shining as the sun,
We've no less days to sing God's praise
Than when we'd first begun.

…

John Newton (1725-1807)

****

Four

Brother-in-law Ben

Lesson Learned

Death doesn't always immediately bring people closer.

There are five years separating my sister and I, she being the elder. Age was not always the main difference between us.

We shared a room all our lives until she moved away for post secondary studies when I was thirteen. I don't think I had ever celebrated a day as much as that one.

It's not like we hated each other, at least I don't think so. It's just that we had absolutely nothing in common. She was shorter, dark and pretty. I was a tall, gangly tom boy. She always had a stream of boys hovering about her, hoping she'd give them a moment's notice. Boys thought I was one of them.

She was beautiful. She had the grace of my father's mother, our Indonesian grandmother and the most beautiful woman on the face of the earth. My sister looked just like her.

Flawless skin. Jet-black hair that cascaded over her forehead in a way that made it look like she'd spent hours getting ready in front of a mirror.

She required absolutely no makeup to look radiant and strikingly beautiful. A head-turner, that's what she always was.

And she dressed to the hilt. Always in the latest fashions from Ella Lynne's, the ladies clothier in our small Northwestern Ontario town. I wore hand-me-downs. Not hers, sadly, because they would never have fit my gangly, long body. I wore all the cast-offs from my two older brothers.

The biggest difference between my sister and me was that she had never been wrong in her life. Next to her, I thought I had never been right. With five years of experience between us, I always felt too small or too tall. Too dumb, too naive, too slow, too fast, too something that was not what she indicated was the right way to be.

I'm sure in my youthful insecurities it was all emotions and interpretations that I had conjured up, but regardless, she had a way of voicing her opinion that always made me feel small and insignificant.

So growing up and sharing a bedroom with her was not the easiest for either of us. As much as I should have developed a thick skin, I was a sensitive softy and often found myself quietly sobbing into my pillow with hurt feelings.

I stumbled through my insecure adolescent years while she was a leader in the high school, winning awards for her athletics and academics. She had a million friends and in her final year at school she fell in love with a boy a couple of years her senior.

Their love continued through their years of post secondary study. She in Winnipeg, Manitoba and he in Ottawa, Ontario at a helicopter pilot school. Shortly after they finished their studies, my sister and her high school sweetheart married.

Their life was destined to be adventurous. First living in

the Northwest Territories of Canada, having a baby and then heading across the ocean to a life in West Africa, where he flew a helicopter for the World Health Organization.

We wrote each other occasionally during those years, my sister and I. This was long before computers and text messages. We did it the old fashioned way, with paper, pen and stamps.

I respected her, was proud of her, loved her, but still never really connected on a deeper level. There just always seemed to be something that kept us from being really good friends.

Not thinking too deeply about it, I assumed it was because of the age difference and the geographical miles between us.

After a year or two of life on the African continent, they came home, stopping for a few months in the town we grew up in. Shortly after their first Christmas season getting reacquainted with snow, my sister and her husband decided to drive out to the Canadian Rockies to ski. They packed their van and headed on yet another adventure, this time with their daughter, my sister's brother-in-law and sister-in-law in tow.

Half an hour from home on their return trip, a logging truck, which was a common sight in those northern pulp and paper towns, lost its load while maneuvering a corner on the highway. Logs became dislodged and flew through the air, hitting the van they were in, killing their brother-in-law instantly.

My sister had serious internal injuries. Her daughter survived unscathed, but her husband was in a coma with serious head injuries. The couple was airlifted to the better-equipped hospital in Winnipeg.

After a few days of heroic measures, my sister's husband succumbed to his injuries while she lay in intensive care, just down the hall from him.

He had never regained consciousness. They never said

goodbye.

My mother, father, two brothers, and I flew to her bedside immediately and sat with her day and night. When she was awake and aware of what was happening, she was so sad. Her heart broke for the man she had loved since she was a teenager, and she mourned the life they would no longer have with each other.

We would rub her back or hold her hand. Sometimes we'd read to her as she slept. I remember the day of his funeral. It was held back in the home town, a four hour drive from the city to which she was airlifted.

As a family we decided that my two brothers and father would drive to the funeral and my mother and I would stay behind at the hospital with my sister. She needed someone there that day to comfort her and hold her as she struggled not only with the death of her husband, but with the pain of her own serious injuries.

It is an assumed thing that death makes people bond on a deeper level. Certainly that was what I always believed until then. In truth, it doesn't always work that way.

I wanted to be my sister's go-to person. I wanted so much to be her equal, to be able to hug her and comfort her and be welcomed into that very big and very hurt heart of hers.

That never happened, though I had wanted it so badly. We didn't get any closer to each other during that time. Although I was confident in all other areas of my life, around her I was still that gangly, awkward little sister.

That was many years ago. My sister has moved on to a productive and wonderful life. She eventually remarried and has two more children who are beautiful and successful.

Our friendship and respect of each other grew with each passing year, but our closeness never had a chance to really build. We have always lived thousands of kilometers apart and have seen each other only sporadically over the years.

I am no longer gangly and no longer insecure. I no longer feel any lesser than any other human being, least of all my sister. Most important of all, I no longer blame her for the disconnection between us all those years ago.

What I learned from my brother-in-law's death is that you can't rush things. Just because someone dies doesn't mean you can impose your own agenda onto someone else's life, especially someone who is grieving.

Things happen as they are supposed to. I believe that with every ounce of my body. It was important for both my sister and me to live very separate lives before I was ready to accept her as she was, and she accept me for who I am, too.

We have discovered something by not pushing our relationship before it was ready. I have found that she is amazing – a loving, beautiful person who makes good and healthy choices for herself and her family.

And she has discovered that I am completely different from her and that's okay. I have accomplished my own things, have my own interests and do things my own way. Although I may not have followed any of her youthful advice, she's proud of the person I have become and I am equally proud of her. Our friendship and closeness is now where it should be.

The lesson was learned.

The cycle complete.

I moved on in my journey of life.

****

Death is not the end
Death can never be the end.

Death is the road.
Life is the traveler.
The Soul is the Guide

...

Our mind thinks of death.
Our heart thinks of life
Our soul thinks of immortality.

... Sri Chinmoy

****

Five

Vivienne

Lesson Learned

Sometimes it's easier to love someone when they are gone.

She was one of the first people in my life that I didn't automatically warm to, and I admit it threw me for a loop.

I always had this knack for making a good first impression. Within minutes I could be the teacher's pet, the favorite friend or the life of the party. So using all my usual social skills and having them absolutely fail was a bit of a shocker for me.

Unfortunately she was the mother of my latest boyfriend and shrugging it off in hopes I'd never see her again was impossible.

She was pretty cantankerous. Those close to her lovingly advised me not to let her ruffle my feathers and not to let her get under my skin.

Problem was, she did. Every chance she got.

In the beginning I was drawn into her arguments, always feeling defensive, like I had to prove my point, which never agreed with hers. She was loud and strong-willed and fought with a tenacious vengeance. Losing the first couple of bouts proved one thing: like a knockout in a boxing ring, she could take me down any time she wanted.

As a survival tactic I did my best to avoid her. It was calmer that way. I rarely spoke in her presence, knowing that silence was the best way to stay out of her firing range.

If her family saw that side of her, they never said as much, at least not to me. She loved her children more than life itself and I had seen her, on more than one occasion, fight like a momma grizzly bear when she felt someone was attacking one of her cubs.

She sure did love her kids though. Around them she came to life, always laughing, smiling and joking. I've heard through the years that she was a wonderful friend too, always fighting for the rights of those she held close to her heart.

Her family was a direct departure from mine. I grew up in a socially responsible, somewhat hoity-toity family where social graces and decorum were paramount. We were never allowed to sleep past ten, could never leave our stuff lying about and were absolutely NEVER allowed to do something as classless as lie down on the sofa.

In my house, dinner was served precisely at 5:50 every night, in the dining room, with china, silverware, and a tablecloth. My parents had their one-and-only pre-dinner cocktail as soon as my father arrived home from a busy day in the office. My mother seemed to flourish when following everything listed in her imaginary rulebook.

Vivienne followed no rules and quite frankly it appeared that no one in her family did either. Not that my family wasn't fun and loving, but her family was fun-loving. There's a difference.

Her family seized every chance to get together for a party. And boy could they party! I still remember my first Christmas with them. My parents were spending that Christmas with my sister, whose husband had died the year before. So my boyfriend and I headed to his parents' home at

9:00 am and by 11:00 am we were all pretty ripped. There was champagne and orange juice with breakfast, bloody caesars, the Canadian equivalent to a bloody mary, with the present-opening time, and more drinks served till half the people needed a nap before the dinner hour.

My mother called to wish me a Merry Christmas and I felt like I was back in college. One hand over my bleary, blurry eye for steadiness, my voice slowed to a crawl in a concerted effort to stave off the slurring. Sadly, I have no memory of what we discussed.

I loved Vivienne's family. I loved mine, too. They were polar opposites and I enjoyed those very aspects immensely.

Eventually my boyfriend and I married. I will never forget the single, solitary compliment Vivienne has ever uttered to me. We had gone to the town courthouse and were married by a Justice of the Peace. Shortly after he had declared us husband and wife, Vivienne walked up, grabbed me in a hug, and whispered in my ear.

"You are the best thing that has ever happened to my son, and you will never hear me say this again."

She's right, I didn't. But in that moment I knew she meant it and in her own way she did love me and was happy I was part of her ever-growing family.

Part of her cantankerous demeanor was blamed on her health issues. By the time I came on the scene, her heart disease was full blown and in those few years I knew her she was in hospital numerous times after suffering heart failure.

It was no surprise that her heart would often fail. She could get herself worked up into a tizzy about this or that and although I am no doctor, I don't imagine all that anger was good for the ticker.

In the end, her heart disease won and she passed away in hospital from congenital heart failure. Even in death her children and husband were all she needed or wanted. I distinctly remember my husband going off to the hospital with only his siblings to say their final goodbyes, while I stayed home with baby in arms and another one on the way.

The first time her spirit came back to visit me took me by complete surprise. Two years after her death, almost to the day, I was in hospital delivering yet another baby. My third.

We decided we'd go as natural as possible with this delivery in hopes of avoiding the long, difficult recovery I had from forceps deliveries with the boys.

Just as the baby was about to make a grand entry into the world, an unplugged machine standing idle in the corner made the oddest clanging sound. I immediately laughed and said to my husband that Vivienne must be in the room because it sounded like the old school bell she used to ring while in the stands at all of her boys hockey and baseball games.

I told the story to everyone in the room about her school bell. The nurses looked up and smiled. So did the doctor.

Vivienne was always tenacious. Gosh that girl never gave up if she had something on her mind and wanted it done.

The unplugged-idle-machine-in-the-corner clanged again. And again and again and again, to the point where everything and everyone in the room stopped. The baby stopped coming. The doctor stopped whatever he was doing down there in the nether region of my body. The nurses stopped. My husband and I both stopped.

We all looked at the unplugged-idle-machine-in-the-corner as it sat there clanging away.

The doctor asked why it was making that odd noise he had never heard before. The nurses were speechless and couldn't answer.

I started to cry and I looked up at my husband and told him that indeed his mother must be in the room. There was no other explanation for this oddity to occur.

I'll never forget the look on the faces of those attending to me. The doctor looked up, with tears welling in his eyes, and made a comment about it being a miracle of birth.

The nurses were crying, wiping tears on their sleeves.

I was sobbing, knowing that Vivienne had come to watch her first son deliver his first daughter into the world.

She has visited me many times since then, and although it seemed odd, even crazy in the beginning, I have gotten used to it. Sometimes I can actually see her. Sometimes I just hear her. Most of the time, though, she comes when one of her children or grandchildren is in need of comfort or direction and it seems as if she's nudging me to help out.

We don't argue anymore. She's still just as feisty on the Other Side as she was here in her earthly life, but she's never angry, pushy or demanding. Instead she has become this beautiful, angelic spirit and I treasure the moments we have together.

I learned from that death that love can grow and build long after someone has passed away. That love, if allowed to blossom, can be a most amazing addition to someone still living an earthly life.

Vivienne and I have become friends, which is more than I ever could have dreamed of.

The lesson was learned.

The cycle complete.

I moved on in my journey of life.

****

I am ready to meet my Maker. Whether my Maker is
prepared for the great ordeal of
meeting me is another matter.

… Winston Churchill

****

Six

Grandparents

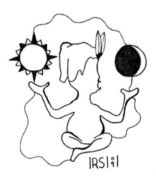

Lesson Learned

It is possible to feel the loss of people you never knew.

There was never a time in my childhood that I missed knowing my grandparents. They had all pretty much died before I was born. What you don't know, you don't miss.

My parents immigrated to Canada from Holland in 1953 and it was here they settled down to raise a family. With my father working in the forest industry, we moved many times from one small Ontario town to another.

The six of us, that is. My parents, two older brothers and the older sister I shared a room with.

We never had huge family meals with aunts, uncles or cousins, unless someone flew in from Holland for a vacation. That only happened every few years at most.

So I never knew what it was like to play with cousins, receive birthday gifts from aunts or sit on the lap of a grandparent who read stories to me. We knew no better and I certainly did not miss it.

I was aware that my friends had all of these things, but not once did I long for something I did not understand.

Truth was, the last of my grandparents died when I was four. I never met him. I can remember living then in Port Arthur which later became half of Thunder Bay. A man came to the door, as I recall, and handed a telegram to my mother. It simply stated that her father had passed away.

I remember standing there, watching her cry. Having no connection to the man who was now dead, I didn't relate to the tears of my mother. I watched her cry with a complete lack of understanding as to why this letter would upset her so. Death of a family member was too foreign to a girl of four tender years.

For the longest time I didn't even know their names. My parents would tell me if I asked, but I would soon forget. Even now, I have to look at the family tree to jog my memory of the names of my forefathers.

And so life went on, the six of us doing everything together without the need for more family members.

Eventually I grew up, married and had children of my own.

I would watch them interact with their grandparents, sitting and reading together, painting, playing, singing. It all seemed so natural and loving and it is here that I finally mourned the death of my own grandparents.

Watching my kids love and be loved, I realized that this was what I never had as a child. I didn't yearn for it to be different. I didn't want to change history and go back to meet my own grandparents, but I did take that moment in time to think of them and wonder what they would have been like.

I realized that although I never knew them in life, it was indeed possible to mourn their deaths many, many years later. It was wonderful to feel this as it allowed me the opportunity to pay tribute to the parents of my parents and all that they had accomplished in their lives.

The lesson was learned.

The cycle complete.

I moved on in my journey of life.

****

I'm Free

Don't grieve for me, for now I'm free
I'm following the path God has laid you see.
I took His hand when I heard him call
I turned my back and left it all.

I could not stay another day
To laugh, to love, to work, to play.
Tasks left undone must stay that way
I found that peace at the close of day.

If my parting has left a void
Then fill it with remembered joy.
A friendship shared, a laugh, a kiss
Oh yes, these things I too will miss.

Be not burdened with times of sorrow
I wish you the sunshine of tomorrow.
My life's been full, I savored much
Good friends, good times, a loved one's touch.

Perhaps my time seemed all too brief
Don't lengthen it now with undue grief.
Lift up your hearts and peace to thee
God wanted me now; He set me free.

Author Unknown

****

Seven

Death of a Dream

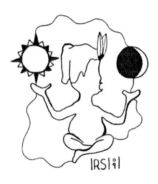

Lesson Learned

Mourning the death of a dream is as painful as mourning a physical death.

Life doesn't always go the way you expect it. I certainly believe in setting goals and working towards those goals, but there must always be flexibility to change your direction, even when you don't want to.

These direction changes are often out of our control and the sooner we accept that a higher power, be that God, the Creator, the Universe or whatever you name it, is actually in charge, the sooner we move forward on our soul journey.

The younger of my two brothers has three children. All beautiful, all individual in their likes and dislikes, and all deeply attached to my heart.

I remember distinctly when his third child, Rebecca, was born. Right from the start she had that sparkle in her eye that always made me think she had a special quality all her own. It was as if she knew the answer and the rest of us weren't even aware there was a question.

I remember my brother and his wife worrying when

Rebecca reached the age of fifteen months and was not yet walking. It seemed so odd to me that they were worried; after all, their older daughter Elizabeth wasn't walking until she was eighteen months. I too had a son who was a late walker, so in my mind the genes were to blame.

Try as I might to put their fears at ease, they felt they needed to consult with doctors. The testing was invasive and I still remember to this day the exact words of my brother when he called with the news.

He said they had been brought in to the doctor's office to discuss the test results. When they were comfortably sitting, he with Rebecca on his lap, the doctor told them the following:

"We have good news and bad news. The good news is that we have a diagnosis of why Rebecca is not walking. The bad news is that she has a disease called spinal muscular atrophy (SMA). It's degenerative. She will lose all muscle capabilities that affect walking, crawling, sitting, swallowing and breathing. There is no treatment, no cure and no hope. Fifty percent of all children diagnosed with SMA will die before their second birthday. Take her home and love her."

When the words ebbed from my brother's lips and I listened on the other end of the phone, tears streamed down my cheeks. They wouldn't stop flowing for many months to come.

Life doesn't always go the way you expect it to.

When babies are born, the family members that love them automatically start to dream of the lives that will unfold. We dream of them being smart and beautiful. Successful and happy.

I had all those dreams for my children just as I am sure my brother did for all three of his. It's the way parents are, it's what we do.

After that diagnosis we entered a dark phase in our lives. It was hard to feel attached to the future without fearing that Rebecca could die at any minute. Because we knew very little about SMA, it was hard to plan and dream as nothing seemed nearly as relevant as the thoughts of losing a child we all loved so very much.

Days passed. Weeks. Rebecca's condition didn't seem to worsen, but still we cried and feared the worst. Learning that SMA was genetic, and knowing as a result of Rebecca's diagnosis that my brother was a carrier, I too went for testing.

Those results came back and with a heavy heart I discovered that I was a carrier. Although it was obvious the disease did not affect my children, because of my carrier status each had a fifty percent chance of also being a carrier.

The thought that more SMA babies could be born and lost in our family was devastating and added to the pain that tore daily at my heart.

The only thing that saved my sanity during those months was the fact that I was training for my second marathon. A 42.2km (26 mile) run that for most people is done just because. Only the top-rated runners actually make money at it, and the rest of us pay to be in the race. Those of us that love marathons *really* love marathons. Most others think we are just plain nuts.

I had just finished my first marathon when the diagnosis came down. Thankfully, my dear friend Janis registered me to race the Chicago marathon the following October. That event hung in front of my eyes like a carrot dangling from a stick before a horse, pulling me through what I later called the days of diagnosis darkness.

Luckily for me we trained five days a week. That meant five times I had to get up, lace the shoes and run. Five times I attempted to run the pain out of my heart.

When my feet hit the pavement there is a peaceful rhythm that balances my body and soul. I have long said that while running I put my mental, emotional and physical exhaustion into balance and when finished for the day, when the shoes are taken off and the water bottles emptied and cleaned, that's when I am at peace.

It's like I talk to God, out there on the road. In the quiet place of the rhythmic movement I ask my questions and I get my answers. Everything makes sense on the run. I no longer yearn for the impossible, yet I know that because I run the impossible is merely steps away, always within my grasp should I want it.

I cried almost every training run as I prepared for Chicago. Janis was unbelievably understanding. Sometimes I talked. Sometimes I just ran. Sometimes I cried. She accepted this stage of my life and adjusted to my needs as we went.

I thought about Rebecca a lot during those runs. How she would never run. How she would never know the joy of feeling her feet hit the pavement in the soft, floating action of a long, slow weekend run. Then I would cry.

I thought about her life and I thought about her doctor-predicted pending death. I wondered how it would feel to let go of something so wonderful, so beautiful and accept that indeed this was part of God's plan. Then I would cry.

I would think about my brother and his wife and how difficult it must be for them. To live with and love a child more than life itself, knowing that every day could be the last. Then I would cry.

I would write angry speeches in my head to God. I would recite these over and over until I wanted to scream at the unfairness that life had bestowed upon us.

We were good people, I would yell to those that occupied space in my head. I would scream that we didn't deserve this, and I would ask why couldn't this happen to some awful people who were mean and needed to learn a lesson. Why us, I would beg. Then I would cry.

Training for a marathon, at least the way I do it, takes about four months. As we approached the end of our training period a shocking and life altering tragedy occurred.

9/11.

Two days later was Rebecca's second birthday. She had reached the milestone that fifty percent of the children diagnosed with SMA don't. It felt too disrespectful to celebrate, considering the pain that was emulating from the tragedy in the United States. So I did not.

Roughly three weeks later Janis and I loaded my car and we started our odyssey trip to Chicago. We were staying with my friends Rick and Anne. In light of what had occurred with the terrorist attack, it was nice to be able to hug our American connections and give thanks that they were not affected personally by 9/11.

The border crossing from Windsor, Canada to Detroit, USA was surreal. The lines were long and it seemed as though every possible security measure was being taken.

I inched the car up towards the customs agent who was standing in the little cubicle-sized booth. She asked all the normal questions; all the while dogs were sniffing our car trunk and back seat. Important-looking men walked around the vehicle hunting for terrorists, bombs or whatever they feared was packed beneath our running shoes.

My attention came back to the customs agent as she continued with the questions.

"Do you have any fruit?"

Looking down at the banana on my console and knowing it was in full-sight range, I hesitantly nodded. I was hesitant not because I knew it was wrong to take fruit across, but more because I liked eating a banana or two the day before a race. And I couldn't help but think of the inconvenience I would now face, having to stop at a grocery store looking for a replacement.

Slowly and with regret in my voice, I uttered, "I have a banana" and pointed to it cradled in the console.

"You are not allowed to bring a banana into the United States of America," she stated rather matter-of-factly.

Darn, I thought. I *really* want to keep this banana.

"Unless," she continued, "it is grown in Canada."

I slowly turned my head in her direction and stared at her in disbelief. Janis hit my elbow to keep me from making a wisecrack about the huge banana plantations we're known for in our tropical Canadian climate.

"Well?" she said, looking exasperated with my delayed response.

Try as I might to be honest, all the while desiring to keep my Central American-grown Chiquita banana, I mumbled, "uh…ya… on the Canadian plantations."

Janis hit me on the arm again and gave me the death-if-you-say-another-word look.

'Well that meets with our restrictions. You can go on through,' declared the customs official, who I was certain by now had never passed a geography test in her life.

The bomb-sniffing dogs were just finishing up and the terrorist-hunting important-looking men, who seemed oblivious to the discussion between me and the customs agent, were wrapping up with their extensive search for whatever they thought two forty-year-old women would have in the trunk of a car. Thorough as they were, they didn't catch the banana, those important-looking, terrorist-hunting men. Nor did the bomb-sniffing dogs. So we two renegade women drove off feeling somewhat like rebels with our undetected contraband banana.

I ate it shortly thereafter. Got rid of the evidence, so to speak.

The Chicago marathon went without a hitch and it was a personal best finishing time for both of us. Well, almost without a hitch. I wore the wrong shoes.

Around the one-hour mark I started to feel pain in my feet. Instead of looking down and allowing the pain to beat me, I sucked it up and ran.

Another thirty minutes later my feet felt like they were on fire, the soles burning and blistering under intense heat. Being honest with myself, I had never, ever had my feet feel like this in a race or training run before. Again, I sucked it up and continued.

Two hours in and the pain was unbearable. I finally

looked down. To my astonishment I had my hack-around-town shoes on instead of my New Balance 762 running shoes. Obviously I had forgotten to change them before heading to the start line.

You have no idea how much making a mistake like that can screw you up in a race. But what was I going to do, sit and cry about it? Stop the race? At that point the Kenyans would have already crossed the finish line and headed to the showers, so it was hardly an option to ask for a re-start for the rest of the 37,000 who were still on course.

Instead I decided that I would just keep running. The physical pain of a few blisters was not nearly as bad as the emotional pain I had been enduring since Rebecca's diagnosis.

So I ran, just like Forrest Gump.

My feet were bloodied, blistered and sore when I crossed the finish line. But it was a personal best finishing time and during those hours on the road I had plenty of time to think about life.

It doesn't always go the way you expect it. But you can't stop living and you can't stop dreaming just because your direction seems to have changed.

I learned in that race that all the inspiration Rebecca brought to me to run faster, stronger and better was actually a little too self-serving. It seemed, for lack of a better word, selfish to me. I vowed that I would continue to be inspired by her, but that I would return the favor and do something, anything to make her life better.

From there the Rebecca Run for SMA was born. A race. A running event to raise money for SMA cure and treatment research.

With humble beginnings and a blind-leading-the-blind management style, I gathered friends and family in hopes I could inspire them to give time and money to my cause.

As it turns out, this event was the catalyst for change within our family. Our entire family, actually – my side, my sister-in-law's side and every friend along the way.

It gave us something positive to do. It gave us forward action rather than sitting stuck in the grieving position. We still worried about the future, and we still feared losing Rebecca too soon, but planning the race gave us an outlet to release our emotions and our fears.

We finally moved forward. We finally started to laugh again, and the dreams of finding a cure began to add a positive energy to us and our desires. It was nice to come out from under the black cloud and acknowledge there was a world out there and it was still spinning.

That was seven years ago and so much has changed. Rebecca is now nine years old. She's in a wheelchair, but holding her own. Although her scoliosis is worsening, and her leg muscles have completely atrophied, her lungs were actually stronger this year, which is a milestone we celebrated.

She's a smart young girl, top of her class in school. Very artistic with her sketching and drawing, a skill that seems to run in my side of the family.

The Rebecca Run for SMA completed its seventh year this past summer and I proudly say we have raised over $1.2 million dollars in the events inspired by Rebecca. Even more exciting than the money raised is what the international SMA research team has used it for.

We now have treatments that help improve the day-to-day life of a child living with SMA. We have FDA-approved drugs that seem to maintain a level of strength in some children. Most exciting of all was the 2007 announcement that the research team had entered into a human trial with a compound so promising; in the mice-testing stage it eradicated all symptoms of disease.

Rebecca continues to inspire me in many aspects of my life. Especially when it comes to finding the positive in everything that happens as we journey through our years.

Life doesn't go the way we always expect it to. But that

doesn't mean it's wrong or bad or that we did something terrible to have caused the pain. The universe works in mysterious ways and it's best to acknowledge there are bigger plans at hand than what we face on an individual basis.

Take Rebecca. Certainly the diagnosis was devastating. I won't sugarcoat that. But we have had so many wonderful things and people added to our lives as a result of the diagnosis, that we must sit back and give thanks for that, if nothing else.

We have been able to create an event, a moment in time where the community comes together for the greater good and to make a positive impact in the quest to cure a disease.

This has become our chance to have an impact in this world, to make it a better place. To save lives. And that is something I not only honor, but am humbled to be a part of. It's a gift and although I would have much preferred that Rebecca have never been diagnosed with SMA, it is what it is and given that we weren't offered a say, I am grateful for everything that has happened as a result of that dreadful diagnosis day.

The lesson was learned.

The cycle complete.

I moved on in my journey of life.

****

Dream

Why do you come to me?
Why do you enter my subconscious
when it serves no purpose?
Why do you visit in the night
when I slumber?

I do not understand the
obsession.
Like that of
a young love-sick child.

I ask – if there is no today
and there is no tomorrow
then go away.

Go back to yesterday

and stay there,

neatly packaged

where you

belong.

But do not cross

the line

into my

life.

I have no place for you

in this time

I currently call

home.

Unless

there is

tomorrow.

… Louise Smith

****

Eight

Fergie

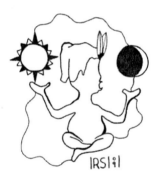

Lesson Learned

Choosing life or death of another soul is incredibly painful.

I don't think I'll ever own another dog.

Not that I don't love them, I do. Not that I didn't adore the dogs I had, I did.

When I was growing up, my parents never granted our wishes to have a family dog. Been there done that, my mother would say, and she'd recount the stories of Sally, their long-before-I-existed German shepherd.

When our youngest child was four years old, I finally made the plunge and brought a bundle of puppy joy home. Hayden, we named him. I had done extensive research on breeds and breeders so there would be no surprises with behaviour and health.

I was instantly hooked into the dog world and ended up socializing puppies for the breeder on a regular basis. For the better part of five years we always had a little bearded collie pup running around the house.

The kids were young then and loved those years. Bearded collie pups are bar none the cutest in the world. A bit of a biased opinion maybe, but we all felt the same.

Eventually we decided to bring a pup over from England. She had great bloodlines and sounded perfect. We called her Fergie.

I fell in love at first sight. Oh my, this girl was special. She had the perfect personality, playful and adoringly sweet. Our bond was immediate and in all honesty I had never felt a love for any four-legged creature as deep as it was with Fergie.

With each passing day I fell more and more in love with my little English girl. She could brighten any day, lift my spirits if they were low, and bring such joy to the simple elements of life, like sitting on the swing reading a book, her head resting on my lap.

When she became ill I spent whatever money was required to keep her healthy, happy and in our life. There came a time, though, when she was five years old that keeping her in our life was more for me than for her.

I knew I had to let her go and I hoped and prayed that when her time came she would slip gently into a final slumber all on her own.

Things don't always turn out the way you hope.

I didn't like doing it. Making the call to the veterinarian. Setting up a time to end Fergie's life here on earth. I hated it.

My heart ached. To me it felt like I was playing God or something, choosing when a life should end.

I had experienced much death in my life up to that point, but this was the first time I felt the odd connection to making the choice.

I knew it was irrational to feel this way. I knew it was best for Fergie as it would alleviate the pain and suffering she was in. I knew millions of people before me had done the same thing.

I also knew the vet would be caring, wonderful and the entire final moment of Fergie's life would be beautiful, restful and peaceful.

Still I was tormented. Making and going to the appointment made me feel sick to my stomach and I just couldn't make peace with the who-am-I-to-decide-life-and-death emotions that tore at my heart.

I did it though. I hugged her tight. I stayed long past the appropriate time a person should sit with their dead dog. And I cried for six months.

A year almost to the day after putting Fergie down, I had to make the decision all over again and put our old, blind Hayden down. He had gone senile and it was best.

I don't think I'll have another dog.

With SMA in my life, I have enough birth and death around me (see Death of a Dream) that whether I want it or not, I am continually connected to that life and death decision.

When we first started the Rebecca Run for SMA, it was all about my niece and our need to find peace with the disease. That very first year another family came to participate in the event. Their little boy was also diagnosed with SMA and this was our first time meeting people who were living our life.

He was a chubby baby, with big round cheeks and stunning blue eyes that could melt even the coldest of hearts. I fell in love just looking at him and was thrilled to meet others who just *knew* what we were going through.

Three months later, weakened by pneumonia brought on by SMA, little Liam passed away in the arms of his mommy and daddy. He was my first SMA death and it devastated me.

It's an ugly disease. It's only seven years since Rebecca was diagnosed and sadly I know more babies that have died from SMA than have lived. I'm not jaded, nor angry. It is what it is.

Liam. Abby. Jamie. Sonja. Max. Ava. Jacob. Allison. The list is endless.

We have become dear friends with many of the parents of these SMA angels and although there is much sadness at the loss of their children, we also share many joyous moments, like the birth or adoption of new SMA-free babies.

In all of this joy, I still think from time to time of the final days in their SMA angels' lives. And I think of the difficult decision to pull the plug that many of them faced.

I struggled with making that decision for a dog. I can't even begin to imagine making that decision for a child.

There is absolutely no way I can compare the two, but in an odd way, I understand the pain these parents faced. Somehow it connects me on a deeper level with them.

I thank Fergie every day, as losing her the way I did prepared me for this part of my journey where I require compassion and empathy for those connected to me through SMA.

The lesson was learned.

The cycle complete.

I moved on in my journey of life.

****

Do Not Stand at My Grave and Weep

Do not stand at my grave and weep,
I am not there, I do not sleep.

I am a thousand winds that blow.
I am the diamond glint on snow.
I am the sunlight on ripened grain.
I am the gentle autumn rain.

When you wake in the morning hush,
I am the swift, uplifting rush
of quiet birds in circling flight.
I am the soft starlight at night.

Do not stand at my grave and weep.

I am not there, I do not sleep.

(Do not stand at my grave and cry.

I am not there, I did not die!)

… Mary Elizabeth Frye (1905 – 2004)

****

Nine

Jack

Lesson Learned

*Guardian Angels exist and spirits of our loved ones come
back to visit if we are open.*

There are two kinds of death. The ones you expect and
the ones you don't. Either way it's a shock to your system
when the news arrives.

I'm the youngest of four children, which means there was
always a ton of sibling rivalry going on in our house. Jack,
the oldest, was eight years my senior. He was the one sibling
who seemed to never have an issue with me.

He never thought I was being too dramatic, a sin I was
indeed guilty of. He never thought I "got away with murder"
in my parents' eyes, a favoritism that was evident to the other
two.

I loved it when he was around. With Jack by my side the
other two were a little more tolerant of me and in all honesty,
I got away with even more antics as he kept our siblings at
bay.

He loved me, and I loved him. He hugged me all the time
and I still remember being devastated when he went off to

95

university at age seventeen. I was nine, and it felt like my knight in shining armor had ridden off on his horse to conquer the world and I was the simple peasant girl, left behind hanging on to the memories.

Jack loved the outdoors, and studying and living in the mountains became his true joy. It was no surprise that he established his life there as a geologist and never lived in another place again.

Eventually he married, as did I. He had kids, as did I. Our connections often came while he drove for hours at a time out to the oil rigs. To wile away the boring hours, he'd make phone calls. I always knew when the phone would ring at 11 o'clock at night and Jack was on the other end, that he was getting sleepy while driving and needed company to keep him alert.

So we'd talk, often for an hour or two. Whatever he needed at the time. He was such a gentle soul, always looking at the positive in absolutely every aspect of life. Even the things that make others shiver, Jack would find a way to make it sound good.

He'd often visit our neck of the woods, bringing his wife and two kids. Family was a critical element of life to him and making sure his children knew their grandparents, aunts, uncles and cousins was something that he took great pleasure in.

We loved those visits. He and my other brother are both competitive rebels when it comes to physical competitions. The rest of us would always sit back and laugh as the first challenge was issued. And it always was.

"I bet I can beat you to the raft in the lake, on a surfboard, using a kayak paddle," one would challenge.

The self-refereed race would go off. Best two out of three. Then three out of five. Next the conditions would change to make it even more competitive. The rest of us would watch for awhile, but eventually we went about our own business as the two of them never seemed to end their battles for ultimate physical supremacy.

They were equals really, in most physical activities. We watched them challenge each other to jump off thirty foot high cliffs into unchartered water. We heard about their antics in the mountains when trying to out-prove who had the most nerve to jump or ski off a rocky ledge.

There were only two differences in the physical abilities between my brothers. The younger of the two was a better mountain biker. He has the risk-taking nerve of Evil Knievel when it comes to barreling straight down a mountain with nothing but a helmet to protect his life.

Jack was a better skier. In fact, he was the best skier I have ever known. Watching him glide down the slopes was like watching poetry in motion. Effortless it seemed. Floating. Surreal. Although I didn't get much of a chance to watch him ski in recent years, I still recalled how it was he that first taught me to maneuver down the slopes at four years of age.

By the time I was six he was taking me with him whenever he went to the small-town ski hill. I remember being too little to hold the tow rope, so Jack would hold me between his legs and with one hand firmly on the rope and the other tightly around my waist, he'd pull me to the top of the hill.

He loved it that I had no skill to turn or stop. Rather than worry about my inability in these areas, he taught me how to use that speed to make it down the hill faster and straighter than anyone else.

And I did. So little and yet I would barrel down those hills, Jack beside me laughing with absolute glee that I could do it. Then back up we'd go. Those days he'd even help me make my picnic lunch so that we could stay at the ski hill all day together.

Sometimes he'd head off and ski on his own and I would stand silently waiting at the foot of the hill for him to come around to my rescue and take me back up.

His friends figured this out and it was not uncommon for one of them to grab me by the waist, hold on to the rope and pull me up for Jack. I was glad they helped as I loved to race down the hills more than anything, but secretly I always wished it was Jack who would whisk me up.

The call came in late on a Saturday afternoon in early May. Almost six years ago.

On the other end was the younger of my brothers and he was crying. It took me more than a few minutes to get out of him what was happening, and when I finally understood the words he was saying, my heart broke and my life changed forever.

Jack had died. At the young age of forty-nine he had suffered a massive heart attack while skiing at Lake Louise in Banff, Alberta.

Jack was the epitome of health. I often recounted stories about how he could climb a mountain and still have enough gusto to play a tennis match after. So it was difficult to understand how he could have died in such a manner.

As the story goes, he had skied with his daughter two days earlier, knowing she was headed out to her summer job as a camp counselor. She shared with me days later that it was during this time she told him that the two of us, his daughter and I, had cooked up a plan to run the Vancouver marathon the following May. She was studying out in Victoria and it just seemed like something we should do.

Then, after a wonderful day with his daughter, he took another opportunity to hit the slopes for a sunny day of spring skiing, this time with his son.

I know Jack. He would have loved being on the slopes that day. Loved it with a capital L. The sun was shining, the weather warm and with little winter gear needed, he would have effortlessly glided down the expert slopes.

I can almost picture what happened next. I can see him, a smile a mile wide, the sun glaring off his white teeth. I can imagine he was thinking that life didn't get any better than that. That's what the mountains meant to him, that's what skiing meant to him. And to share two days with his kids on the slopes, I can bet he thought he was the luckiest man alive.

I can bet he thanked whoever his God was for the privilege to be there in that moment of time. And I imagine that it was then that God called him home. His job on earth complete. His lessons learned. I can even imagine that Jack would have thought that was the single best way to die, if one had to.

His son, skiing with a buddy, saw a person being attended to by the Ski Patrol while they rode up on a lift. He had no idea that it was his father and that the man he looked down upon was already dead.

Not long after, the Ski Patrol found my nephew and told him the news. The police helped him home, an hour's drive away. Phone calls were made, including the one to me.

Once I was off the phone, I knew that the hardest task of my life lay before me. One that no matter how much I wished I could be exempt from, it was only right that it was I who did it.

I had to tell my parents.

I drove to their home and waited by the curb for them to return from a social evening. At midnight they arrived home. I walked up their driveway and asked them to go inside. Although I am deeply spiritual I'm not religious at all, but still I prayed a little as I prepared myself to deliver the news.

It was to this day, one of the most difficult things I have ever done. I knew with conviction that the moment the words ebbed from my lips, their hearts would break and would never heal again. I wished and wished that I didn't have to tell them, that I didn't have to say those dreadful words.

I sat them down, pulled a chair up in front of them, held their hands and with tears welling I whispered, "Jack died today of a heart attack."

Then I just waited for it to sink in. I kept holding their hands. Mom gasped a little, questioned me a few times.

Shook her head in disbelief. Eventually it sunk in and we all cried.

My other brother arrived. He drove the hour from his place to our parents' like a madman just to be with us. We talked, cried and made our plans to fly to Calgary as soon as possible.

People flew in from all around the world to pay their respects. Who knew that Jack was that well liked? People came from Ireland, France, Holland, Australia and all over Canada. It was good to be with the family and friends. It made the process of saying goodbye a little easier.

Eventually we all came home and went back to our lives. I thought about Jack every single day. It was Rebecca Run season, the time of the year where I volunteer endlessly on the race (mentioned in the chapter Death of a Dream).

One day, about three weeks after Jack had passed away I was driving on the highway, coming home from a press-approval for the Rebecca Run participant t-shirts. I was thinking about all the little SMA children that had passed away. I was wondering if in death they knew about the event and if their spirits would come back to visit us on race day.

Then Jack came. Right in the middle of my thoughts, his image appeared in front of my face, transposed like a veil on top of the images outside of my windshield. His image was clear as a bell.

Startled, I said, "Jack?"

I saw the image nod. I shook my head, cleared my eyes and again said, "Jack, is that you?"

Again he nodded.

With tears streaming down my cheeks and a feeling that some sort of higher power was keeping me safely moving forward on the highway, I talked to him.

I thanked him for being a wonderful brother. I told him how sad we all were and that I wished I could have seen him one more time before he left.

He nodded.

I asked him if he would be at the Rebecca Run and if so, could he keep an eye on all the little SMA angels that would be hovering about.

With his signature smile a mile wide, he nodded.

Shortly after this his image evaporated and I was left alone with my thoughts. I didn't care that it seemed crazy and I didn't care what other people might think. I simply thought it was Divine that Jack had come back to me on the road that day.

We have spoken many times since his death. Sometimes I ask him to come; sometimes he comes on his own. It's always peaceful, calming and a privilege.

I don't think I have any skills that anyone else doesn't have access to, and I am not certain why it happens so easily for me, but I treasure every single second I see Jack and am blessed that I feel him nearby much of the time.

It wasn't long after his first apparition that Jack's daughter and I talked via email. She had discovered that the Vancouver marathon would be almost to the day of her dad's one-year anniversary of passing. And to the surprise of both of us, the charity of choice was the Heart and Stroke Foundation.

We ran the race and it was spectacular. It was an epic trip on so many levels. I flew to Calgary and then my sister-in-law, Jack's widow, and I drove through the mountains out to my niece in Victoria.

We all did the race, each at our own individual pace and alone in our thoughts. It was a tribute race for me, and I dedicated each of the first 41 kilometers to a year Jack and I had together. My job was to remember something specific from that year and that in itself made the race fun and the kilometers pass quickly.

Those that have run with me before know that I have issues with the porta potties. Not that I don't like them, just that there never seem to be enough for me.

I marvel at the world record holders that never have to

jump off the race route and relieve themselves in a johnny-on-the-spot or a protective bush, both of which are often my best friend along a long-distance race route.

It's not like I can hold it, out there on the race course. Sadly, when I have to go, I HAVE TO GO!

Many a time I have run a race with nary a port-a-pottie in sight. You have no idea how exhausting and painful it can be to hold your bodily functions. As such, I have often run off course, into gas stations, restaurants, back alleys and even the odd ditch, just to relieve myself so that I could concentrate on the run again.

Like in most races, that day I had to relieve myself often. But a miracle occurred and I will forever thank Jack for making it happen.

Every time I even thought I might need to go, there appeared immediately along the route, a sparkling clean port-a-pottie. Each one smelled great, was hardly used and much to my surprise had not a single person waiting to use it.

It was like my very own angel of port-a-potties was leading the way, making sure my needs were being met instantly. Remembering how Jack had carried me up the ski hill all those years ago, I knew it was him, my very humorous knight in shining armor, saving the day once again.

After forty one emotional, yet wonderful and healing kilometers, I started the final one. I saved it to represent the year that he was gone. The last year, since his death.

During this kilometer I recounted the difficulties in losing him and the lessons I learned as a result. This is often the hardest kilometer physically in a marathon and it just seemed fitting that I went through the tough emotions in those final moments along the route.

I made peace with everything that day. Although I would much prefer he still be alive, it is what it is and I feel lucky to have learned that people do go somewhere fabulous after they pass, and that they do come back to visit those who are open to being visited. Knowing this and believing this is something I will cherish for the remainder of my life.

I also learned he was still my knight in shining armor, now with a new title, my guardian angel, for nothing less than that could have put together an instant-as-you-need-it line up of port-a-potties for 42.2 solid kilometers of a marathon.

The lesson was learned.

The cycle complete.

I moved on in my journey of life.

****

"I believe that we all decide when to leave our physical body and 'go home' or 'join God.' I don't think most of us are aware of this choice on a conscious level, although some people who are highly attuned to the spiritual world, including children, sometimes are. But mostly, it's a subconscious 'knowing' of the soul that it's time to leave this realm and move onward to the next one.
Perhaps we've learned all we're capable of learning or need to learn here, and understand it's our time to 'graduate.'
Or perhaps our leaving also involves teaching other people left behind important lessons of their own that they'll learn as a result of our departure."

… John Edward, *The After Life* (Princess Books, 2004)

****

Ten

Death of a Marriage

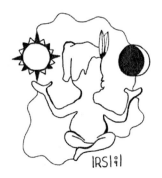

Lesson Learned

The five stages of grief apply, even when it is a relationship that dies.

So far I am one of the lucky ones. Never say never, but thus far my marriage of twenty-two years is holding strong.

Certainly we've had our moments. Any marriage would. But I am a glass-half-full kinda gal and can always find the positive in any situation. It doesn't hurt that I am married to a pretty nice guy. He's loving, supportive, a good father and is easy to spend time with.

Others are not so lucky.

With the divorce rate for North America being somewhere around the fifty percent mark, everyone is bound to have a friend or family member call their marriage quits at some point.

I seem to have a zillion friends who have walked these miles. Although I am no psychologist and have absolutely no training in marriage counseling of any kind, I seem to get asked for help all the time. As such, I have given this subject some deep, unqualified thought.

One thing that seems consistent in every story I have heard, is that the end of a marriage is much the same as a death. The stages of grief exist and both husband and wife will have to go through all of them at some point.

The five stages of grief are:

1. Denial and isolation,
2. Anger,
3. Bargaining,
4. Depression, and
5. Acceptance

Stage number one in the death of a marriage is denial and isolation. It's when most married people stop listening to their "gut" or intuition and instead listen only to their logical-thinking head. They probably feel in some way that there is a problem, or the end is coming, but try to ignore it as best as possible.

I have seen friends who detached themselves from their spouse for years before finally moving forward. Almost always, the one who did all those years of quiet contemplation went through the stage of denial long before the discussion of separating came about.

I've also seen some married couples stay in this stage for ever. Neither one wanting to admit that there are glaring holes in their relationship and as such they fake it.

Next comes anger, and boy does it come. Everyone goes through this stage, some when still together, others after the separation.

It's the stage where people let things the other half does irritate them. When that irritation starts, it's often intuition kicking in and subtly letting the person know it's time to move on. Many ignore those move-on feelings and just stay mad.

It's a stage where each partner will say and do things they later regret. Frustration gets the better of everyone at this point in the death and it seems to come out in anger directed at the other half.

When my friends have gone through this I have always given a piece of advice. Keep it civil and legal. And know that this is just your intuition telling you to move on, so move on. Quit fighting it as it's just making it harder on everyone around you.

The third stage of bargaining is rather interesting, from a lean-on-my-shoulder-dear-friend perspective. I've had friends come up with all kinds of wacky ideas to keep their other half in a dead marriage. Even when they are not happy, for some odd reason they just can't get themselves to let go and they promise to change, improve, almost anything just to make the other happy.

I remember a million years ago my college love dumped me rather suddenly. We had spent the better part of two years together and had talked marriage and post-studies employment. All the things young couples in love talk about.

There were problems near the end, but I happily lived in stage one, denying my gut feelings that we were heading towards a breakup.

When he dumped me, over the phone no less, I was devastated. Cried for hours like any young gal would. Then I started to bargain. I called him and promised the world. I would change this and that, do this or that. I said anything and everything I could think of in hopes it would spark a tiny bit of interest in getting back together.

He didn't bite, thank goodness. Although in that moment of grief I thought my world would end, about a month later I realized that indeed the relationship wasn't good anymore and indeed it was time to move on.

I realized that although I had loved him before, I didn't anymore. That was the point when I made it through all five stages of grief and could move on in my journey of life and love.

That's always odd to me. Couples who are not happy or are downright miserable together and still one half of them comes up with all kinds of bargaining ideas to save a marriage they don't actually like much.

With a human life there is always birth and death. The two constants. You can't have one without the other, ever.

In all my years of watching marriages start and sometimes end, I've come to the conclusion that sometimes they are *meant* to end. Not everything has to go on for ever and ever and ever, especially when they are exhausting your energy, killing your joy and leaving you drained and miserable.

Our society tells us differently. It tells us that a marriage is for life. But I don't see it that way.

I believe in fate. I think everything happens for a reason. As such, I know every marriage that takes place serves a purpose for those two souls. But maybe the lessons from that union are learned quickly. For our soul to keep moving towards our true destiny, we are best to acknowledge that we have learned lessons, the marriage is no longer required, and it's time to move forward on our journey.

Sadly, far too many don't do that. Maybe they stay in the angry stage for so long they no longer remember what it was like not to be fighting.

Sometimes they try and try to keep the marriage intact, maybe for the kids, maybe for financial reasons, or even for this or for that. I've had a friend stay miserably married because she feared being alone. She was stuck in that place with no forward movement in her soul's journey for what seemed to be forever. That was sad to watch.

Or sometimes the jilted half can't move on and bargains and bargains and bargains. To the point that they veer so far off their own path that they no longer know who they are and what they want out of life.

Then there is the final difficult stage of depression. Almost always from my perspective those that are *thinking* of separating before informing the other half go through this depression stage before that discussion takes place. The other half generally experiences this stage after separating.

Sadly, I have seen people stay stuck here in the depression stage far too long as well. They mourn and mourn the loss of what once was. They bargain, they beg, and eventually they just melt into a heap and then sadness follows them everywhere as they attempt to live life.

Acceptance is the final stage of grief. For most it eventually comes but, sadly, not for all.

There is no set of rules for grieving the loss of a marriage just as there is no set of rules on grieving the death of a loved one. There only seems to be these stages, these periods of time that range from moments to lifetimes depending on how those who are affected cope with the loss.

I'm no expert, but having had so many friends and family go through this particular type of death, I can say the following:

* There is something bigger at play than any moment in time any one person will experience individually. Even though it might feel like it, this isn't just about you! The sooner you accept that, the easier this experience will be.
* You can't change what another person says, does or thinks, so quit trying. You can only change your reaction. Knowing this means you control what you say, do and think. Take the high road. Life is too short for anything else.
* Don't feel bad after the fact if you say and do stupid things in the bargaining stage. I can remember saying idiotic things that were downright embarrassing after the fact when my college love dumped me many moons ago. What is said in the heat of the moment when your heart is hurting the most should never be held against you, so stop feeling guilty. Letting go of everything, even the memory of your crazy actions and words, is essential to moving forward on your journey.
* If you are angry, acknowledge that you are merely in the angry stage of grief and remember to keep everything you do and say legal and civil. Don't do or say anything that

can be held against you in a court of law. The sooner you let go of all the million reasons why you are so mad, the faster you will move on. Yes they hurt you/spent too much/had an affair/embarrassed you/bankrupted you/ran off with the neighbour, whatever. You're not the first person this has happened to and although it feels like you are raging inside, the faster you let it go, the better off you will be.

❖ You are no longer with them so quit obsessing about their life. Their soul has its own lessons to learn and path to follow. Staying attached to them just means you are stuck yourself. If you've ever seen those old Western movies, when someone gets stuck in the quicksand, rarely do they ever get out. So don't step in it. And those of you reading this that are saying 'ah, but there are kids involved, I have to stay connected to their life', please go back and re-read the second bullet point. You can't change what your ex does, says or thinks about his/her involvement with the kids. You simply need to change *your* reaction and then move forward. You can only control yourself.

❖ Make a list of the things you *do* want in your life. As soon as possible after the separation has become apparent, start making a list. This is your chance to acknowledge the things that are important to you. Start with the easy things like: I want my kids to be happy; I want this separation to go as smooth as possible; I want my kids to love me no matter what; I want to find peace and contentment at the end of every day. This just allows your mind and heart to focus on positive thoughts during a very difficult time. Trust me, this is much better than allowing yourself to stay busy thinking the world has come to an end. Doing this will also help you traverse the rocky moments in the stages of grief a little easier and possibly quicker.

❖ If you are the one who wanted out, then let the other person go. There is no need for you to hang on any longer. I've seen too many who wanted out, but wanted

114

to still have a say over what the other half did, who they saw and how they moved on in their life. You wanted out, so be out!

❖ Jumping into the next relationship before you have successfully completed all five stages of grief is a problem waiting to happen. It stops you from the very important task of rediscovering who you are, what you want out of life, and what your soul purpose is. I've seen this happen far too many times and never yet has it worked out okay. Usually it fizzles out, and sometimes one of you will make too many concessions in the new relationship that will over time irritate you as much as other things did in the old relationship. In essence you're just repeating the same pattern, the same mistakes, and not learning the lessons that were put before you. Just remember, you can't skip any of the stages of grief, which may happen if you jump into the arms of an immediate replacement. Eventually those stages and those lessons will find you again.

❖ Ask for help. If you are like me and believe there is some sort of higher power, be that God, the Creator, the Universe or simply your Higher Self, then call upon this power to be with you and guide you through the stages. You'll discover you are not alone and no matter what happens you are loved. For those of you reading this who question the existence of something so great as a Higher Power, I'm not sure what to say other than 'good luck with that.' Seriously, with so much death that has occurred in and around my entire life, it naturally stands to reason that I have had to question the existence of something greater than we humans. I am at peace with my beliefs and I encourage everyone to study, question and develop their own. It's a wonderful feeling knowing what you stand for.

I don't envy anyone who has to travel the difficult route of ending a marriage. Not ever having had to do this myself, I can't say what it would feel like to me. I can only offer those that still need to walk these miles the reassurance that this difficult stage of your life will end, as long as you let it.

Acknowledge the death of the relationship, allow yourself to grieve in each of the stages and when ready, look up and forward to the rest of your glorious life.

Learn the lesson.

Complete the cycle.

And move on in your journey of life.

****

To err is human; to forgive, Divine.

… Alexander Pope

****

Eleven

Kudret's Dad

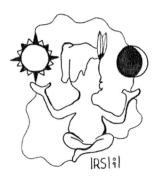

Lesson Learned

Death knows no cultural boundaries and it is a privilege to learn how others honour those who have passed on.

Although I spent most of my childhood growing up in white-Anglo-Saxon, protestant, rural Ontario, I have lived my entire adult life immersed in the most multi-cultural area of Canada. And I love it.

I have friends from many races, cultures and backgrounds. It makes for interesting conversations, parties and definitely eating.

One such friend is Muslim. We don't talk much about religion as it's just not an important part of our friendship. His wife, also my friend, is Catholic, not that that makes a difference to our discussions either.

Early this summer his father passed away rather suddenly. It was a rather tragic story. The father was vacationing in Europe with his wife and died suddenly while on a Mediterranean cruise,

This created an instant international nightmare for my friend, his brother and the rest of the family. I admire how they rallied together, dug deep into their treasure chest of energy and managed to attend to his death in an honorable and efficient manner.

Because they are originally from Europe and that was where my friend's parents were staying for a few months, the brothers took the body back to the home country and buried him according to their Muslim faith.

When it was over and the family members had been attended to, the brothers came home.

I have since learned that in the Muslim faith a prayer service is held in memoriam, forty days after the passing occurred.

Being very good friends, my husband and I were invited.

It was hard for me to contain my excitement as this was my very first time attending anything Islamic. My friend schooled me on the protocol of covering my head, taking off my shoes upon entering the Mosque and having my forearms covered in respect.

Plus I had to remember this was a memorial service and not a full-out, have-a-good-time party. So the excitement I was feeling would have to be toned down. To show my glee could have been misunderstood and that would have been disrespectful on my part.

As we drove to the Mosque, I had time to reflect on my expectations. Westerners always seem to talk negatively about the rights of women in the Islamic faith. Thinking about all that I had read over the years, I fully expected that I would feel a sense of segregation as I was schooled that indeed the women would be separated from the men most of the time.

I also thought I would feel a sense of "beneath," considering the men would sit with the Imam in the prayer hall and the women, covered from head to toe with scarves and clothes, would be relegated to the balcony area, away from the men.

We arrived at the front door and were met by a lovely

lady who was just going in herself.

"Do I cover my head now, or after I am inside?" I asked her tentatively, not wanting to be either disrespectful or intrusive of her space.

With the grace and charm of a caring grandmother, she smiled warmly and helped me with my scarf. She even commented on how lovely it was.

Inside we went and seeing all the shoes lined up near the front door, my husband and I followed suit, placing our shoes in the racks provided and walked forward in our sock feet.

Then we saw our friend. He seemed genuinely happy that we had made the trek down to Toronto to attend the service for his father, a man neither my husband nor I had ever actually met.

After a warm embrace and a slight teasing about my head scarf, he instructed us as to where we were to go, separate of course.

My husband went right. I went left through a hallway, around a corner, and entered into a meeting place. There were long tables set up with chairs all around. The first thing I noticed was that only women were sitting at the tables. All with heads covered, all looking up at me with warm smiles.

I looked up across the room and spotted my husband on the men's side. Giggling to myself at how we were actually in the same room, only separated by an imaginary line, I lifted my arm and quickly waved to him. He waved back and then we each took a seat on our separate sides, I with the wife of our friend, he with some strangers.

It was hard to wipe the grin from my face. I was soaking up every single aspect of being in this place that was so culturally different from anything I had experienced before.

My original expectations were that I would feel *lesser* or *beneath* by having my head covered. Quite the opposite was actually the truth. I didn't feel below or lower. Instead I felt an incredible sense of equalization with all the other women. Once the heads were covered, there seemed to be no judgment based on income level or value of clothing. There was no division based on education.

We were all equal. All women. All there to recognize the life of a man. To pray and honour his soul as it passed to wherever the Islamic faith says souls go upon death.

Soon we were called to prayer, which meant the men then left the visiting area and entered the prayer hall. The women, walking down a separate hallway, went past the prayer hall and up the stairs to the balcony. A balcony that was separated from view of the prayer hall by a beautiful fabric drape.

Soon the Imam began. What he said I do not know, as it was all in Arabic and Turkish. He chanted in such a beautiful rhythmic way that I found myself slowly and easily drifting to the peaceful calm of his voice.

Being a long-distance runner and cyclist, I am used to the wonders of a rhythmic sound. I often have the same effect from hearing my feet hit the pavement, each step in perfect harmony with the previous. Or my breath while riding. Drawing in and releasing, making my own music that calms my heart and heals anything that may be out of balance.

Not understanding a word of what was chanted was absolutely irrelevant to me. I just sank back into my self, listening, breathing and feeling immensely at peace.

Another strange realization hit me while sitting with the women, segregated from the men during the prayers. I felt a strength in numbers. A powerful sense of connectedness to all the women sitting together.

In our silence we were one. Far greater and far stronger than any one of us alone. There was an energy growing around our collective group and for the first time in my life, I felt an incredible power building, just because we were women. Equal women, as determined by our covered heads.

It was mesmerizing, calming, empowering and wonderful all at the same time. When the service was over and the Imam quiet, I was sad. Simply because the moment had ended and I knew in all likelihood this would be my last chance to experience the greatness and wonder of an Islamic ceremony.

The women all filed down the stairs and back to the meeting area. The men did the same, following their own pathway. Food was served. Conversation flowed. Eventually a few men sauntered closer to the invisible line separating the genders. Women shyly did the same, me included, all the while careful not to disrespect the customs required in the Islamic Mosque.

When it was all over and I was about to bid farewell, I smiled contentedly, knowing that it was a privilege and a blessing to be part of something so beautiful.

I said my own little prayer to Kudret's dad, letting him know how special I felt to be a part of his memorial prayer service and I thanked him for teaching me the valuable lesson about the joys to be had by celebrating in another culture's traditions.

The lesson was learned.

The cycle complete.

I moved on in my journey of life.

****

"Believe nothing just because a so-called wise person said it.
Believe nothing just because a belief is generally held.
Believe nothing just because it is said in ancient books.
Believe nothing just because it is said to be of divine origin.
Believe nothing just because someone else believes it.
Believe only what you yourself test and judge to be true."

… Buddha

****

Twelve

Near Drowning

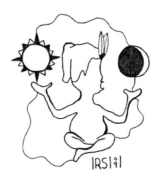

Lesson Learned

Our time to die is our time to die, whether we think it should be or not.

In all of my life of doing crazy things, being a bit of a rebel and taking chances that would make my mother quiver, I had never actually had a near-death experience. Not until this past summer.

I can remember riding my bike across the highway as a thirteen year old, playing chicken with the transport trucks that barreled by. I think I knew that they would win, if it came to that, but being dared by my friends was such an adrenalin rush that I never said no.

I remember crossing the train tracks to get to the other side of town, never caring in the slightest if there was a train in the way. Sometimes I went under, sometimes over, sometimes while the train was moving.

I can remember thinking about the better crossing option when the train was moving, just in case it picked up speed. I wondered if it would be better to be under the train, lying flat against the tracks until it had gone by, or would it have been better to be on the hitch that connected two cars, jumping off into the ditch on the other side. I usually chose under, never letting it occur to me that crossing the tracks while the train was moving was a stupid thing to do.

I can remember at eighteen years of age, barreling down a mountain while skiing in the Canadian Rockies with friends. On a dare I went down a run that was so beyond my skill I could easily have wrapped myself around a tree or flown off a cliff and ended my life right then and there.

At twenty I dragged my boyfriend to the New River in Vermont to whitewater raft in the spring run-off. Naturally we had no previous experience and I do recall being washed overboard while shooting a class 4 rapid. Our guide, known as The River Rat, told me later that someone had died in that exact spot the previous year. I laughed at the craziness of it all.

Although I have calmed down greatly, and rarely do anything that could result in death, I still like to challenge myself with physical activities. That's probably why I ended up running marathons and ultra trail races even though I pretty much suck as a speed runner, and ride long distances on my road bike, just to see if I can. And it's probably why after just purchasing a new mountain bike I allowed a riding buddy to take me on the most technical trail in the tract, just to see how far I could push myself.

Having kids must have been what calmed my nerve a little. That and having an über conservative, feet-firmly-planted-on-the-ground husband who would absolutely never risk life and limb in the name of a dare.

So my life is much calmer these days. I enjoy all aspects of nature, specifically running, hiking, trails, cycling and swimming in the cool waters of a freshwater lake.

This summer we were invited up to a family cottage for a few days of rest and relaxation. Having spent the previous three months taking care of business, family and organizing the Rebecca Run for SMA, I did not need to be convinced to sit on a dock and do nothing for a few days.

Family and friends were there and it was such a lovely, easy rest. My husband's brother Luke and I canoed to the end of the bay. The bunch of us toured the lake on the boat. And the rest of the time was spent swimming, walking or lazing about, enjoying anything and everything all at the same time.

Conversation easily flowed during the days and evenings. I don't recall how or why, but one particular evening during dinner we talked about death. I remember distinctly telling everyone that I felt your time was your time and although you could make choices in your life as to the quality of your health, your time was still your time and when your lessons were learned, your soul would pass to the Other Side.

Shortly after this discussion ended, I decided to jump in the lake for a quick and refreshing evening dip. Having grown up in the north where we had our choice of five or six lakes all within a ten minute drive from our house, I was beyond comfortable with lake swims.

I'm pretty strong too, when it comes to swimming. I love nothing more than treading water for hours on end, swimming up and down the shorelines looking at everything from cottages to the natural rugged forests that creep up to the water's edge.

Off I went, alone. I even brought biodegradable shampoo with me, thinking I'd take a northern-girl's shower, which is a quick dunk, soaping up and another quick dunk to clean the suds off.

On my second dive into the lake, I looked up and noticed two things. One, there was a huge bush blocking my view of the upper deck where my family and friends were relaxing. Two, Luke's ten-month, eighty pound lab jumped in the lake to join me.

I had swum with her earlier in the day and calmly welcomed her to join me again. Besides, it was I who had taught her how to retrieve a stick from the lake and as such we had bonded rather nicely.

In her excitement to see me, she got just a little too close for comfort. While treading with both legs and one arm, I used my other arm to gently hold her back from coming any closer. Using soft yet stern commands from my dog training years, I instructed her to stay back.

In her youthful puppy exuberance, she misread my commands and assumed I wanted to wrestle.

Her mouth went over my arm, her body leapt on top of me and before I had any idea of what was happening, she was wrestling me and holding me under water with her weight.

I now know how strong swimmers can drown in a matter of ninety seconds. Panic set in pretty quickly and in seconds I was hyperventilating while fighting under the weight of the dog.

Numerous times I came up for air, but panic doesn't allow you to breathe properly and going back under immediately meant only one thing: I had even less air in my lungs.

I knew I was completely panicked, and I also knew there was nothing I could do about it. While coming up a couple times I tried to make a sound, like a call for help, but nothing would come out except gasps for air.

All the while I kept fighting the dog to get off me. The more I fought, the more she loved the game and played even harder.

After probably no more than a minute, there was a stop-time moment where everything seemed so peaceful. I could feel myself floating.

I saw there, in that calm and peaceful place, all of my accomplishments in life. They flashed quickly before my eyes and I was glad to have had so many wonderful memories.

But in that moment, I also knew I was going to die. There was no question in my mind and when I had finished seeing all the wonderful moments of my life, I saw a few things I had not yet accomplished.

I was instantly filled with overwhelming sadness. I distinctly remember thinking, "I got it all wrong. I always thought based on age alone that my husband would die before me. I thought I would see my long-lost, best childhood friend Camille and the town where I grew up. I thought I would see a cure for spinal muscular atrophy. But this is it, and I got it all wrong."

I floated there in that calm, yet sad place for what seemed an eternity.

Then I heard a loud, deep, male voice scream inside my head.

"YOU HAVE THIRTY SECONDS!"

Having these words blast through every ounce of my body jerked me back to reality only to discover I wasn't yet dead but was, in fact, still fighting with the dog. She was on top of me. I had one arm in and out of her mouth. Under the dog's weight I splashed, fought and pushed with my free arm, trying to get away.

Knowing I had another chance gave me a push to do what I could to survive. I silently whispered to the you-have-thirty-seconds voice, "please God let me yell for help, just once."

I surfaced and surprisingly the word HELP flew quickly from my lips.

The rest is a bit blurry. I remember coming up for air once and saw someone diving off the dock. In my crazy I-am-going-to-die mind I remember noticing the person had clothes on and that seemed odd to me.

The next thing I recall is being dragged to the dock by someone who kept asking over and over and over, "Are you okay, are you okay, are you okay…"

I remember coughing and puking water, air and whatever else had become lodged inside my lungs.

I remember being in shock, and everything around me moving in slow motion. I got out of the water. I held a towel. Then I looked back, in somewhat of a daze, towards the water to see who it was that had dragged me out.

There, looking as white as a ghost, was Luke.

Realizing he had just saved my life was so overwhelming that for the first time ever, I could not form words of gratitude. They hovered there in my throat, but try as I might, I just could not utter a single word. I couldn't even look at him.

I stayed affected by the near-drowning for a few days. As soon as I came home, I sat quietly in my office and with tears streaming, penned an email to my long-lost childhood friend Camille.

I couldn't tell the kids, though, or anyone else for that matter. I just couldn't talk about it as tears came often and for no reason. I knew I needed help to heal from the trauma and so I set up an appointment with my homeopathic doctor who is also a reiki specialist and a shaman healer.

The first thing she noticed during my healing meditation was that my spirit was only half in my body. She asked if I had experienced the feelings of speaking with people or doing things and at the same time watching myself speaking or doing. This described to a tee exactly what the days following the near-drowning were like for me.

She called in the Divine and all of the great healing forefathers. During the meditation, they assisted in patting my spirit back safely into my body. The moment the meditation was complete I felt whole again. Together. All of me as one.

Shortly after I was able to tell my friends, family and children about the event, and that too felt cleansing and right. I happily report that I was also finally able to give my thanks to Luke for saving my life.

Although I had intended on telling him verbally, it felt more appropriate that I send him a note with my thoughts and feelings hand written, so that we could both heal completely from the event in privacy and move forward in our lives.

I still believe that our time is our time. I believe this is written into our soul's journey long before we are actually born. I believe that all of our souls have lessons to learn and tests to pass in this life. As such, we are put into situations and live the lives we live, all in hopes of learning whatever it is the soul has mapped out as essential in this journey of ours.

And when we are done, when all the lessons that were meant to be learnt are complete, we will head home to the Other Side, to our loved ones who have passed before us and to God, and the spirits and angels that accompanied us with guidance and support throughout our life on earth.

This particular near death, although it certainly felt like it in that moment, was not my time. It was merely a wake-up call to move forward in a few aspects of my life. Like seeing my long-lost, childhood friend Camille and the town we grew up in.

It also prepared me for the many more death-related occurrences that came up in the following weeks, which all eventually led to one single place. Here. At my desk writing this book about death and the lessons I have learned.

I feel drawn to write these words, as though there is a greater meaning to everything than I currently know.

I look up at the monitor, read what was written, and know with conviction that the words that ebb from my heart are indeed meant to help others heal and move forward in their own soul journey.

Difficult as it is to believe that these words may help those I have never met, I give thanks that all of these death-related experiences have occurred in my life so that others may grow, connect with their soul purpose and reach their own individual destinies.

The lesson was learned.

The cycle complete.

I moved on in my journey of life

****

Red Fox

On a cold and rainy fall evening,
Red Fox felt the jitters.
She circled the den,
counting the pups.
Four had not returned from
their playful romp.

Red Fox sensed danger
lurking about.
A danger so great,
even she
couldn't hide
behind one of her many
disguises.

Rather than bolt

in fear,

and alarm all in the Great Forest,

she slowed her breathing,

laid quietly in the dark,

and waited for danger to pass.

From the depths of the cold and damp den,

Red Fox knew in her heart

that one of hers

would not

return.

… Louise Smith

****

Thirteen

David

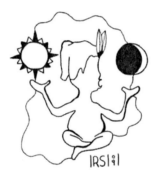

Lesson Learned

Whether you know the end is coming or not, you have a choice to make - get busy living or get busy dying.

My brother-in-law David died this summer. Two weeks after I almost drowned. One week after the prayer service for Kudret's dad. It was a summer of death. The catalyst for writing this book.

David had cancer for six years.

There are so many things I learned from both his illness and his eventual death that it's hard to capture in just one lesson. The wounds are also still so fresh and the reflection period that I normally maneuver through following a death is not yet complete.

From the moment he was diagnosed with cancer, the relationship between he and I changed. Although his wife, the sister of my husband and I have always been extremely close, more like sisters than in-laws, David and I never really bonded any deeper than required for a typical family social gathering.

Not that I didn't like him. It was probably based more on

the size of the family. He and I just never found the time to sit one-on-one when we were all together.

That all changed after his diagnosis. Afterwards I remember having deep conversations with him, mostly about life and living. He never seemed too interested in talking about the severity of his prognosis, death, finality or anything like that. But he did like talking about his beliefs in regards to "being busy living, not busy dying."

That was what he did. He stayed busy living to the best of his abilities right to the very end. He stayed positive, engaged, working and even though the bone cancer was tremendously painful, he never let that stop him from enjoying the every day aspects of being alive.

Because he was so busy living, we, the extended family never really talked about the end. We just followed his lead and kept busy living, loving every single time we got together for a large-scale family gathering.

Although I always knew deep down what was eventually going to come, the phone call took me by surprise.

David had been admitted to the hospital and was not expected to come out.

Following his own "busy-living" philosophy, he had worked on the Thursday. Was in far too much pain to do much of anything on the Friday, Saturday or Sunday.

On Monday his daughter-in-law went into labor and delivered a healthy baby boy. David was in too much pain to go and see him.

Tuesday morning, as he stood in the bathroom, his chin dropped to his chest and when he was unable to move his head in any way, he called his wife for help.

In the hospital later that morning, doctors confirmed their fears. The bone cancer had eaten away at the vertebrae in his neck and as a result it had snapped in two. David remained in good spirits, even joking about his new neck brace.

Wednesday his daughter-in-law was released from the maternity ward. With tears streaming down her cheeks, she walked into the elevator and rode up to the palliative cancer care ward. There she introduced her son to his name-sake grandfather.

Moments later David deteriorated and drifted into unconsciousness. That's when the calls were made.

The next day I was honored and privileged to be with my sister-in-law-call-me-sister and the kids when David passed to the Other Side.

Immediately I went into work mode, taking care of the death-related business details, all the while trying my best to say and do the right things for the family.

Another sister-in-law and I made the arrangements. We organized the Celebration of Life. I, having much experience with keynote speaking and facilitating, acted at the request of the family as the master of ceremonies. I wrote and delivered the family eulogy.

I'm not quite sure how I held it together during that time frame. Looking at the sorrow on the faces of his loved ones tore painfully at my heart.

In times like these you never know what to say or do. You wonder if anything helps at all. Rather than rely on my own human logic, I trusted the entire time to Divine assistance. I would meditate at night and in my head I would simply ask that the right words and actions flow from my body and lips.

It was, without a doubt, a very difficult stage for me in this journey of life. It is still raw and I don't often have moments of thinking about my niece and nephews, or sister-in-law-call-me-sister without tears welling in my eyes.

Each time, I am reminded of David and his desire to be "busy living, not busy dying," and it warms my heart knowing that he taught me this lesson.

There is no rule on how long a successful life should be. There is no rule on what signifies success. For me it all comes down to this.

Your soul determined your life lessons long before you

were born. Your role in this life is to learn the lessons that are then put before you. Complete each cycle, pass the tests and move along on your journey in the direction of your destiny.

A destiny your soul chose before you were born. A destiny that will remain a mystery to you for your entire life until your final cycle is complete and you pass to the Other Side.

For so many human reasons I wish David had lived. To know his new little grandson. To walk his daughter down the aisle one day. To see his youngest son settle into a career. To grow old with the woman he married over thirty years ago and loved deeply right to the last day.

But spiritually I can't help but celebrate in the knowledge that he did it all. He learned all of his lessons, passed all of his tests and reached his destiny. There is nothing greater than that. Than knowing a soul has done everything it set out to do.

Birth and death. The cycle of life. We cannot stop it from completion, nor should we attempt to. Rather we should cherish each moment we have, look for the lessons in everything and give thanks for each step we walk on our journey.

We can only hope that when our time comes to pass to the Other Side, we leave an impact that benefits the beautiful world left behind.

The lesson was learned.

The cycle complete.

I moved on in my journey of life.

****

Tribute on the passing of a very real person.

People are of two kinds,

and he was the kind I'd like to be.

Some preach their virtues,

and a few express their lives by what they do;

that sort was he.

No flowery phrase

or glibly spoken word of praise

won friends for him.

He wasn't cheap or shallow,

but his course ran deep,

And it was pure.

You know the kind.

Not many in life you find.

whose deeds outrun their words so far

that more than what they seem, they are.

Author Unknown

****

Epilogue

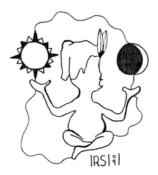

My sincere apologies if any information represented in this book is incorrect. The stories are merely memories from my life, the way I remember them. Many names have been changed to protect privacy.

Two stories in this book focus on spinal muscular atrophy (SMA), the disease that affects my niece Rebecca. For more information on the events founded in her honour, please visit:

www.rebeccarun.com
www.angelgala.com

For more information about SMA and the research being done in Canada, the United States and internationally, please visit:

www.fsma.org
www.CureSma.ca

Acknowledgements

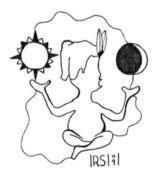

I have had amazing friends and family over the years and this book exists because of their love and support.

The tales I tell are written from my perspective, and although I may not have seen some of you in years, I thank you for walking the journeys with me:

Darla Ciolfe, Laura Weston, Camille Robichaud-Cox, Blair McDonald, Georgina Turner, Marjorie Smith, Rebecca van Fraassen, Doug and Theresa van Fraassen, Janis Jarvis, Barb and Jim Hirsch, Fergie, Marinus Adriaan Maarten (Mark) van Fraassen, Mary and Kate van Fraassen, Glenda Colucci, Kathi Van Son, Kudret and Cathi Buyukozer, Don and Kim Smith, Asha Frost, Debbie Ballantyne, Doug, Gail, Ryan, Lindsey and Blake Pullin.

Supportive of every step I take, my husband Paul, and children Eric, Richard and Sydney. My parents Adriaan Maarten and Grietje van Fraassen, and niece/dear friend Sarah Ballantyne.

The always-supportive Smith and van Fraassen clans – without your love my life would be empty.

The grandparents I never knew, Marinus Adriaan Maarten van Fraassen, Marie Louise van Fraassen-Ornek, Joris Molenaar, and Meindrina Clasina Molenaar-Knoester.

The SMA angels that grace me with their spiritual presence, Abby Loebach, Jamie Haapalainen, Sonja Stefanovic, Max Vallender and Liam Zajdlik.

To my friends that volunteer relentlessly on the Rebecca Run, you have blessed my life in many ways, and it is an honour to know and work with each of you.

Special thanks to Camille for the week away from life which allowed my mind-chatter to stop and the thoughts for the book to form.

Also thanks to Stephen Semeniuk for sharing the story of his dad's passing while we rode road (cyclist-speak) on a late-summer day. In that precise moment I went from *thinking* I might write the book, to *knowing* I had to.

Michelle Morra and Judy Penz-Sheluk, thank you for your editing, professional advice, and uplifting words of encouragement.

Sydney and Janis, thank you for sharing your photography. Richard, thank you for your drawing titled *The Journey*. I love you!

Asha Frost, thank you for being the beautiful healer that you are. My success in completing the cycles is largely due to your guidance. You are a gift!

To all those who influence me in ways you may never know, thank you.

And finally, to the wonderful Divine support that made all of this possible. Without the continuous love and guidance from the Great Spirit I would be just another soul wandering aimlessly through my human life.

About the Author

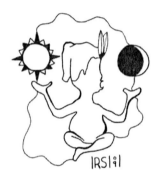

Louise Smith is a gifted speaker with an uncanny ability to hold an audience completely enraptured, regardless of whether her tales focus on business, running, cycling, spiritual growth or making a difference.

Balance is a key ingredient and Louise finds this in cycling (road and mountain), hiking, and running nature trails for hours at a time. The soft rhythmic action, along with the peace and calm in a forest, create a perfect opportunity for her to talk with God.

With a successful communications and corporate training career under her belt, the summer of death and the 2008 crash in the economy forced Louise to reckon with the lessons placed before her and flow with the current once again.

Guided by the love of writing and her need to make a difference, www.TheLessonsOfLife.com was launched with the purpose of helping others find their way when the path seems a little murky.